The Classic Best-seller

A Salesman's Guide to

More Effective SELLING

Dedication

This book is dedicated to my wife Mildred and to our children, Barbara, David, Louise, Robert and Nancy and their families who have practiced effective win-win selling techniques on me and each other over the years.

It is also dedicated to the members, past and present, of the National Society of Sales Training Executives who have unselfishly shared with me over the years, their high-level knowledge, skill and experience in training professional salespeople for major corporations of the United States.

A Salesman's Guide to

More Effective SELLING

by Homer Smith

Marketing Education Associates
4004 Rosemary Street, Chevy Chase, MD 20815

This book is available at special discounts when ordered in bulk quantities. For more information, contact: **Marketing Education Associates,** 4004 Rosemary St., Chevy Chase, MD 20815. (301) 656-5550. E-mail: **homsmith@erols.com**

Copyright 1998
All rights reserved
Printed in the USA

This is a reprint of the classic best-seller by Homer Smith, *A Salesman's Guide to More Effective Selling,* originally published by the Book Division of *Sales & Marketing Management Magazine.* When S&MM discontinued book publishing, *Marketing Education Associates* took over the publishing at the request of companies who regularly over the years have given copies to their new salespeople as part of their training in *basic selling techniques.* The current trend in sales training of "returning to the basics" of persuasive win-win selling called for a revival of this quick-study, how-to classic salesman's guide,

Library of Congress Card Number 88-92440
ISBN 0-9621285-0-3

Contents

Chapter

Chapter

INTRODUCTION

There are hundreds of books on selling. There are many sales courses developed for schools, business firms and for self- study. If salespeople could read the right books and take the right sales courses, they would certainly do a better job of selling. But the typical salesperson doesn't have the opportunity or the time to select and read all the books or take all the courses. And this is fortunate! Yes, fortunate! For if salespeople could, they would be so utterly confused by the volume of facts and differing opinions that they couldn't sell!

Several years ago, Sales Management Magazine, (now Sales & Marketing Management) recognized the great need for a digest of the best of selling techniques to help salespeople quickly develop a logical, effective selling plan. They selected Homer Smith to write the book, a national sales training director for a major office machines company with a reputation for identifying successful selling techniques and teaching them in a clear and concise manner. The result was *A Salesman's Guide to More Effective Selling*.

It's a basic selling how-to book with all the fluff and padding removed. It's for new salespeople who need to produce quickly and profitably, and for older salespeople who want to do better. A reviewer for a major business magazine called it "the Reader's Digest of the best in selling techniques."

The book was an immediate success with major as well as smaller companies who bought copies for all their salespeople. One international business machines corporation with a reputation for leadership in training salespeople, after reviewing the book, bought 2,000 copies for distribution to all their branches. In the years since its first publication and through several reprintings, previous buyers have regularly reordered copies for new salespeople.

Because *A Salesman's Guide to More Effective Selling* has earned the title, *A Classic*, we decided to reproduce it in its original form to avoid any dilution of its power. Since it was first printed, many theories promoting unique selling terms and formulas and requiring complicated psychological analysis of the styles of salespeople and their prospects, have come and gone. Today the trend among professional sales trainers, like members of the National Society of Sales Training Executives, is "back to the basics" in selling techniques.

A Salesman's Guide to More Effective Selling has certainly stood the test for basic selling principles, so for the many past users who asked for another printing . . . here we go again!

Women are "Salesmen," too!

A Salesman's Guide to More Effective Selling was published just before pressure developed to differentiate between the sexes when talking about the workplace. So we apologize, ladies, for using the terms "salesman" and "he" in a generic sense for anyone in selling throughout the book. It was our desire to reproduce the original book faithfully, so we ask that you assume that whenever the author used the word *salesman* in an illustration, he certainly meant that women in selling could and would do the same.

The author is currently editor of the popular bi-weekly publication for salespeople, *Master Salesmanship*. Even though a poll taken by the publisher before selecting the title showed that most women were not offended to be called a "salesman," he now uses the term "salesperson" to reflect the growing numbers of successful professional women in selling.

The Creative Salesman

T HE salesman is the sparkplug that starts the engines of our great industrial economy and keeps them going. Nothing moves until he makes a sale. All employment, all profits, and even the taxes that pay for government, start with a sale.

No one will deny the genius and contribution of the scientist, the engineer, management and labor who provide the products or services the salesman sells. Without them, he couldn't survive. But he is the one who tells people about the better way, convinces them that they want a better way, and persuades them to try it. By providing the outlet for the fruits of genius and the financial return to pay the bills, he keeps the laboratories and scientists hard at work developing better things for better living.

There is no limit to success for the creative salesman who can discover needs and applications for his product, then persuade people they can satisfy basic desires through buying it. Top salesmen make the highest income of any profession. Some make more than their own company presidents, frequently more than top level management. More and more of the top executives in our companies, large and small, are coming from the ranks of selling rather than from production or finance as was formerly the pattern.

The old-time salesman was characterized as the fast talker, a story teller, flashy dresser, a great extrovert personality. He maneuvered his customers into buying from him through friendship or high pressure. This was the character portrayed by Willy Loman in Arthur Miller's *Death of a Salesman*. But the play symbolized the death of an era of selling while building up to the death of its principal character, Willy.

Today, the growing complexity of our economy, the advances in technology, and the great explosion in new products and services, call for an entirely new kind of salesmanship. And for a different kind of man, with a different outlook and a different background for selling. Some call it the age of the "soft sell," but don't let that fool you. It is planned, intense selling, that solves problems and moves the prospect into a buying mood much more safely than the "hard sell" ever did.

What is "Creative" Salesmanship

A woman walks into a store, asks for a specific item, pays for it and walks out. Was a sale made? Legally, yes. But no *selling* was involved!

The order filler performs a needed function in our sales structure, but he is the lowest rung on our salesmanship ladder. While he is found mostly in the stores where customers come to him, he is also seen calling on regular accounts, taking orders for staple, relatively low-priced goods and services.

Creative selling, in contrast to ordertaking, involves establishing a need, creating a desire to have the need satisfied, and persuading the prospect to use the salesman's proposition as the best method of satisfying the desire. Creative selling can be done in the same stores where the order taker is found. And many of the route men who call on regular customers are selling creatively instead of succumbing to the easy ordertaking — "How many cases do you want today?" — approach.

Any salesman who can talk about his customer's problems can do a creative selling job, inside or outside of the store. But the opportunities for creative salesmanship are greater outside the store, in the home or the office. Here is where we find the higher levels of salesmanship, and here is where the salesman finds the greatest rewards. This is the operating arena for the salesmen of consumer specialties, industrial supplies and equipment, and intangible services.

Professional Salesmanship

Selling is at its highest level when the salesman takes on the relationship of a consultant and advisor to his client, the customer. This is sometimes referred to as "service" selling because the customer solicits the service of the salesman and his firm to solve a problem and the products involved are almost incidental. Like the doctor who examines the patient and prescribes a medicine to make him well, the salesman examines the customer's needs and prescribes a particular product or service that will make the customer happier.

By studying his products and giving generously of his time, knowledge and experience to solve the needs of his customers, the modern salesman becomes a true professional man who is respected for his position and service.

The 4 Great Areas of Competency

To be successful in his career, the professional salesman must be competent in four major areas. He can acquire some of the knowledge and understanding in high schools, colleges and private schools. On top of that, he will be trained by the firm for whom he works. But most of his understanding and techniques will come from self-improvement through study and reading, observing other salesmen, studying people, and intelligent analysis. Here are four areas in which he must develop:

1. **Proper Attitude.** How the salesman feels about selling as a career, about his immediate job, the firm he works for, the products he sells, his supervisors, his associates, his customers . . . all adds up to enthusiasm that is vital to do a successful selling job. Some of these attitudes are affected by outside influences over which he has no control. But once the salesman realizes that his own mental attitude toward making a success in selling is as important as his knowledge and skills, he can make adjustments to his environment.

Perhaps the greatest influence on one's attitude toward selling is training and successful experience. The salesman who is sure of his knowledge, skills and work habits is eager and willing to put this competency to work. His successes soon become more frequent, and his morale increases to the point where he tends to ignore the normal setbacks and minor frictions that come with the job.

2. **Product Knowledge.** Few will disagree that the successful salesman must know his product. But the modern concept of salesmanship emphasizes that pure product knowledge or information is not enough. Emphasis in modern sales competency is on learning the advantages and benefits for the customer as well as the actual features of the products. The typical manufacturer's catalog may do a good job of pointing out and even explaining the features of a product. But now we know that the customer is more concerned with what it will do *for him.* So the salesman must be prepared to translate them into obvious benefits.

In some types of selling, the salesman must have a substantial technical knowledge of a customer's operation as well as of his own product or service. This knowledge, however, must still answer the customer's basic question: "What will it do for ME?"

3. **Selling Skills.** Product knowledge alone, even when learned in terms of customer benefits, is not enough for effective selling. If it were, the baker would be the best bread salesman, and we know this is not true. How the information is used by the salesmen when he faces the customer is equally important. In fact, there will always be the argument between sales experts as to which is more important, product knowledge or selling skills. It will never be settled satisfactorily, but salesmen need not concern themselves with it so long as they prepare themselves in both areas.

Competitive selling depends greatly on the skill of the salesman in:

A. Understanding what motivates people to buy
B. Locating and qualifying prospects
C. Making the approach to the prospect
D. Conducting the sales interview and making good demonstrations
E. Handling objections
F. Closing the sale
G. Building good will

4. **Work Habits.** Many details that lead to success in selling have nothing to do with product knowledge or skill in selling. These include such activities as:

A. Planning the call

B. Efficient utilization of time

C. Maintaining proper records

D. Proper territorial coverage

Proper work habits are essential to close the gap between knowledge of good techniques and selling procedures and the actual use of these assets in the field.

How's Business?

The professional salesman is in business for himself. Sure, he works for a firm that pays him a salary or commission. But he works with little supervision compared with other working people. He uncovers most of his own customers, usually develops some into clients. He frequently works an assigned territory, and all the business he develops from it is his. Instead of plant, inventory and machinery, his assets are time and talent. How he uses them depends upon his desire and his ability to shape his own areas of sales competency — his Attitude, Knowledge, Selling Skills, and Work Habits.

Why People Buy

BEHIND every sale is a buying motive. Nothing is bought without one, yet the customer is seldom aware of why he really bought.

The customer's buying motive is never the desire to own the product itself, but rather to gain something the product will provide. Millions of paper clips will be sold this year and yet nobody wants a paper clip. What they really want is to hold papers together. They don't even buy a particular paper clip because its wire is corrugated instead of straight. They buy it only when they are convinced the corrugations will hold the papers together better.

Wanting to hold papers together is a good enough buying motive for the paper clip salesman. But actually his prospects don't want to hold the papers together so much as they want to avoid the loss in time, money or security that might come if they didn't hold the papers together. Not important, you say? Read on!

Satisfy the Real Need

Everyone has many needs. The number and kind depend on a person's standard of living. He has many needs of which he is not aware, or which don't bother him even though he is aware of them. But there are some that build up a tension within him until they are satisfied. This tension converts the need to a want and then to a desire. Not until this stage does the prospect buy.

Before a salesman can help his prospect buy, he must first understand what that person really *wants* to buy. When he understands what motivates a particular person to buy, he can focus all of his skill, time and effort to supplying those factors in the right quantities at the right time.

You don't have to be a psychiatrist to be a salesman, but you can put to work what the experts have found to be true about all of us.

"Motivation Research" and the Salesman

"Motivation Research" — finding out *why* people buy — is one of the most significant advances in marketing in recent years. Buyers' testimony as to why they buy particular products is frequently unreliable. Some people just don't know why they buy, while others knowingly or mistakenly ascribe their purchases to the wrong reasons. The researchers aim to find the real reasons behind people's purchases. Their findings usually are reported in psychological terms, but salesmen learn plenty from their discoveries.

"So What Does It Do for Me?"

It has been decided that everything we do is related to our own personal interests. Even our actions in behalf of others give us personal satisfaction as a sort of compensation. To the salesman, this means that his prospect will buy only if it is to his self-interest. He is not interested in the salesman, the features of the product or the salesman's company — only in the advantages and benefits that contribute to his personal well-being.

Most of us like to think that our decisions are based on logical thinking, that our purchases are dictated by a balanced consideration of all the facts. While this may be true on occasion, the psychologists tell us that more sales are based on emotional response than on logic. More cars are bought for their styling, for prestige and pleasure than for the efficiency, economy and time-saving they offer as an answer to transportation problems.

Many a hard-headed businessman has bought a certain brand and model of steam iron simply because his wife wanted it and not because he was convinced it would work better or be a better buy than another. Some housewives won't buy a product if one of their neighbors has it, while others buy a particular product because all their friends have it. Don't try to figure it out, just make the most of it.

If the salesman can appeal to logic, he does so, but he brings in all the emotional appeals he can to clinch his arguments. He may point out that a new typewriter will type letters faster than the old one, but he will also stress that the machine will be fun to have around with its beauty and style, that the boss will think the office manager pretty smart to have bought it, and that the secretary will think he's a dreamboat for being so concerned for her morale.

Every Prospect Is Different

It would be easy for the salesman if every person bought the same product to satisfy the same personal desire. But motivation is a personal matter and each prospect determines which benefits and advantages he wants most. Then he buys the products and services that seem to him to promise the most of those benefits for what he can afford to pay.

Factors which shape a person's goals and values, and thus his buying decisions, include his heredity, environment, education, experience, social status, and income. All these affect the strength of the buying motives from person to person.

The person is also constantly changing. Time, immediate circumstances and mood will give a person a special reason for buying or refusing to buy.

Aim for the Buying Motives

What are the motives that induce a person to buy? Sales psychologists do not agree on the number or the terminology, but they are generally in accord on the postulate that everyone strives to attain his or her own personal satisfaction above all else.

In addition to the primary desire to survive, there are six basic buying motives that are popularly accepted. Four are often mentioned in pairs because they are related positively and negatively: Fear of Loss and Hope of Gain; Pleasure and Avoidance of Pain. The other two are Pride and Desire for Approval.

More specific buying motives can be named, and these appear in texts on selling and human behavior. But all of them can usually be placed within the framework of these six basic motives. In the following breakdown, examples of specific buying motives are shown after each basic buying motive. Some are related to two or more. Good health, for example, can contribute to all six motives although it is probably most positively linked to pleasure. That is why the advertisers say, "It's fun to be healthy" instead of, "Save money on doctor bills."

6 Basic Buying Motives

1. Profit or Gain. (Save money; economy; profit).
2. Fear of Loss. (Safety; protect property, health, or loved ones; future security; save time; prevent loss; long wear; guarantee).
3. Pleasure. (Comfort; convenience; enjoyment; admiration from others; luxury; good health; affection; sexual attraction; save time; good food and drink; good housing; beauty).
4. Avoidance of Pain. (Protection; relief of pain; security; less work; safety; good health; no worry; become more attractive).
5. Pride. (Desire to possess; advance in skill; self-improvement; style; beauty; high quality; latest fashion; prestige).
6. Desire for Approval. (Social acceptance; affection; learning; admiration; prestige; imitation).

Understanding Benefit Not Enough

The prospect may fully understand that the product will satisfy one or more of his desires most satisfactorily, and still he will not buy. Why? Sometimes it is because he weighs all the satisfactions he will get from this expenditure of dollars against the satisfaction he will get from the same dollars spent in a different way.

Often several motives war inside the prospects' mind and the strongest ones at the moment will win out. He may agree that your product will give him great pleasure, but fear that the money thus spent will force him to cancel or postpone another project may overrule his willingness to buy. At another time, his desire for pleasure can overrule his fear of loss.

The Salesman and Buying Motives

If the salesman can discover what the prospect really wants and how much, he has the key that will open the sale. A homely bit of rhyme is frequently quoted to bring this important point into focus. It goes:

*"To sell John Brown what John Brown buys
You must see John Brown through John Brown's eyes."*

By whatever means he can, the salesman must determine which buying motives will have the greatest effect on the prospects decision to make the purchase, and which are the strongest ones at the moment. Then he should emphasize the features, advantages and benefits of the product that will best encourage those motives.

4 Ways to Determine the Buying Motives

A salesman must seek his prospect's motives early in the interview. They are related to the prospect's problem and needs, and they can be discovered in these four ways:

1. **Ask questions:** "If I could save you time in producing your invoices, would you be interested?"

2. **Listen for volunteered comments.** The prospect says, "I often wished I had more time to play golf."

3. **Listen to comments during the presentation.** "I wish our old machine would go that fast."

4. **Observe.** Study the prospect, his surroundings, evidences of hobbies, products he now owns.

What to Do About Buying Motives

The average salesman can't expect to know all that is involved in the mental and emotional process that makes a person finally buy. It would be an interesting study, but it isn't necessary. You do have to recognize certain facts, however. This summary may help.

1. The prospect will not buy until he is prodded into it by a specific buying motive.

2. The prospect's buying motive will never be the desire to own the product itself but rather to gain something that the product will provide. He is not interested in the features of the product, but the benefits the features produce. People don't buy color television sets, they buy the pleasure of watching a beautiful picture. Sell the pleasure.

3. The prospect will not buy until he associates the product you are selling with the advantages and benefits that it will produce if purchased.

4. This means that you must present your product in a manner that emphasizes the benefits in which you believe the prospect is most interested. You will mention a feature, a stainless steel part, for example. But you will immediately relate this to some buying motive, like "fear of loss," by saying: "You will not have to replace it later because it won't rust." Don't assume that the prospect can or will make this association on his own. Help him!

5. Finally, you must convince the prospect that the benefits he will gain from buying the product are more important than the loss of the money it will cost. "This small investment will bring you enjoyment for years to come, plus the pride of owning such a beautiful . . ."

Apply the "FAB Formula"

Knowing that the customer buys *benefits* and not things, the salesman finds it useful to convert his product's features into ultimate customer benefits before planning his sales presentation. A handy device for doing this is called the "FAB Formula." The name comes from the fact that it involves the Feature, Advantages and Benefits.

The salesman merely sets up three columns labeled Features, Advantages and Benefits. He writes the principle features in the first column, the *Product Characteristics*. These answer the question, "What is it?"

In the second column, opposite each feature, he writes the Advantages the feature offers. These are the *Performance Characteristics* of the features, answering the question, "What will it do?"

In the third column, he writes down the ultimate Benefit to the customer, the end result. This answers "What will it do for me?".

Here are several examples of how the three-column FAB chart works.

FEATURES (What it is)	ADVANTAGES (What it does)	BENEFITS (End result)
Aluminum legs	Will not rust	Saves replacement cost
Flavored with spices	Tastes good	You will enjoy it
16-ounce bottle	Less cost per ounce	You save money
Vinyl tile	Will not scuff	Less work, looks better
Sculptured carpet pile	High and low design	You'll enjoy its beauty

Use this simple three-column chart to help you convert your product features into customer benefits.

When demonstrating his product to the customer, the salesman often finds more success in shifting the FAB order to get the benefit across more positively. For example, with the aluminum legs feature above, the salesman might say, "These aluminum legs (Feature) will save future replacement cost (Benefit) because they will not rust (Advantage)." He can also put the benefit first, like this. "Your floors will look better and take less work to keep clean (Benefits) because this vinyl tile (Feature) will not scuff (Advantage)."

"So What?"

You will get a better idea of the importance of breaking a product feature down into advantages and benefits if you imagine the prospect saying "So what?" to your remarks.

"This is a 16-ounce bottle."

"So what?"

"It costs less per ounce."

"So what?"

"You save money."

"Oh!"

When practicing, think of the prospect wearing a hat with the words "So what?" printed boldly on it. If you should be giving the benefit first, the prospect will be saying, "Prove it!"

Now you may be thinking that any prospect who doesn't realize that he saves money after you tell him the product costs less per ounce is pretty stupid. Sure, he could figure this out for himself, IF he was intently listening to you all the way. But suppose he happens to be inattentive when you mentioned the cost per ounce. The positive benefit— "Save money!"—would recall him from his distraction and put the sale back on the track again. Don't take a chance. Take another second for insurance. Lead him to the benefit, a basic desire, his real buying motive.

Do that, and you're much, much closer to a sale.

Planning the Sales Interview

E VERY successful salesman plans his sales interview before he faces the prospect. It may take a few minutes — or several days, depending upon the purpose of the call, the prospect, and the product or service.

Like the good lawyer, the successful salesman prepares adequately in advance before he faces the judge, his prospect. It has been said that good salesmanship is 90% preparation and 10% presentation, and this is certainly the case in *creative* selling.

Planned or Canned?

The sales presentation comes in many degrees of planning, each of which has its champions among sales managers. Some firms provide salesmen with prepared presentations which they are required to memorize and deliver verbatim to the prospect. Others provide outlined sales presentations which cover the most important features, advantages and benefits. The salesman memorizes the outline so that he covers all the points, but he fills in the supporting information in his own words. Whatever the plan followed by the salesman's firm, it is usually developed from a study and analysis of the sales presentations of successful salesmen.

But, whether provided by the top management or the individual salesman, the presentation must be planned to lead the prospect up a logical path toward the sale.

6 Stages in Planning the Sale

A number of formulas for selling have gained popularity over the years, and they are being followed by more formulas and modifications of earlier ones as new books appear on the market. We cannot hope to discuss them all, but the salesman will find reading in the fields of modern sales psychology stimulating — and confusing.

Our objective here is to show the basic planning the typical salesman must go through in preparing for the successful sales interview.

There are six basic stages in carrying out the sale.

Stage 1. **Prospecting.** The salesman must find and qualify his prospects.

Stage 2. **Pre-Approach.** He must study the prospect, collect information about him, then plan the sales presentation.

Stage 3. **Approach.** He gets the interview and comes face to face with the prospect. He gets the prospect's attention and interests him in the possibility of satisfying a need.

Stage 4. **Demonstration.** He makes the demonstration of his product or service to acquaint the prospect with its features, advantages and benefits. He stimulates the prospect's desire to have his need satisfied by the product or service.

Stage 5. **Objections.** Sometimes the prospect raises objections to going through with the sale. The salesman expects objections, prepares for them, probes to find them if they are suspected. When they are found, the salesman overcomes them.

Stage 6. **Closing.** The salesman helps the prospect take action that will complete the sale satisfactorily.

We will consider each of these stages separately. Meanwhile, we need to consider what the prospect is doing in his own mind that affects the outcome of the sale.

5 Mental Steps to the Sale

The experts may give them different labels, but most will agree that the steps in any sale boil down to taking the prospect by his mind and leading him through these mental gymnastics:

Step 1. **Attention:** You must get his favorable attention.

Step 2. **Interest:** You must arouse his interest in your propostion.

Step 3. **Conviction:** You must prove his need for your product.

Step 4. **Desire:** You create a desire to satisfy the need by demonstrating the benefits he will receive.

Step 5. **Action:** You help him decide to buy your product, or to agree to your proposition.

Sales presentation planning puts together the talking points, questions and actions which are the ammunition you will use in your battle plan, your sales talk. The salesman gets the necessary knowledge from the product literature, the talks and comments of his sales manager or supervisor, other salesmen, the manufacturer's field men, and from his own personal invention and experience.

The prospect's first mental step in the sale, his *Attention,* opens the Approach stage. Attention-getters are only temporary, however. You must move right along to Step 2, arousing the prospect's *Interest.* In a good sales talk, it's difficult to determine when one step leaves off and when another begins. In fact, during all the rest of the sales call, you must maintain the prospect's attention.

Interest depends primarily on your appeal to the prospect's buying motives. If possible, decide before the sales call why this particular prospect should buy your product or service. This type of planning is sometimes called the Pre-Approach. As the opening of the sale progresses, questions will uncover specific buying motives.

Conviction, identified as Step 3 in the mental process, requires proof to the prospect that he *needs* your product. Demonstration, try-outs, testimonials, surveys, questioning — all may be involved in proving the need.

Closely allied to conviction that the prospect needs the product, is Step 4, *Desire* to satisfy that need. This is generally accomplished with the same selling tools, the demonstration, testimonials, surveys, etc. But it is brought about by taking the prospect mentally into the future to let him visualize himself enjoying what your product will do for him. You point out the features of your product, but you go beyond the simple recital of its qualities and picture the advantages of the features and the personal benefits that the prospect will experience. The technique for doing this was covered by the "FAB Formula" on page 11.

Conviction and *Desire* sometimes come quickly, but most of the time there comes a stage that experienced salesmen call *"Overcoming Objections."* During this period, the salesman studies the reactions to his sales presentation and probes the areas that are not clear or convincing to the prospect. When he finds them, he repeats or reinforces those parts of his presentation intended to create the desire for his product or service. We will discuss the technique for overcoming specific objections later.

The final step, *Action,* is usually called "Closing the Sale." If all the preceding four steps are carried out skillfully, this final step is merely the routine of signing the order, or arranging for the time of delivery.

Closing a sale where all the preceding steps have been executed properly is like getting a girl to say "I do" at the wedding ceremony after a successful courtship.

The 7 Big Buying Decisions

While the salesman leads his prospect through the five mental steps of the sale, he must be aware that the prospect must make seven basic decisions. If the salesman expects to close the sale or get approval of his proposition, the prospect must say yes *to all seven!*

1. Will I SEE the salesman?
2. Will I LISTEN to him?
3. Do I NEED the benefits he proposes?
4. Does HIS product give me these benefits?
5. Is he the best SOURCE for the product?
6. Is the PRICE reasonable?
7. SHOULD I buy?

These decisions may be made in any order, and some may have already been made before the salesman makes his appearance. It is the first job of the salesman to decide which decisions have been made and what the answers are. Those which haven't been answered in his favor he attempts to change. He wastes no time on those which are already in his favor.

Let us consider what the salesman must plan in his presentation to make sure that he can induce the prospect to say yes to each of the seven decisions.

1. **Will I see the salesman?** Get the interview appointment. Create curiosity.

2. **Will I listen to him?** Get attention, ask questions, isolate the need quickly.

3. **Do I need the benefits?** Establish the need through observation and questioning. Make sure that the prospect understands his need and the advantages and benefits of having it satisfied.

4. **Does the product give these benefits?** Appeal to the prospect's buying motives. Pick the features, advantages and benefits which will lead to conviction that your product best satisfies the need. Use demonstration, testimonials, case stories, trials, samples.

5. **Is this the best source for the product?** Establish the service, convenience and reliability of the manufacturer, your firm and yourself.

6. **Is the price reasonable?** Convince the prospect that your price is fair for all the advantages and benefits obtained. This does not necessarily mean that it is the lowest price obtainable! Repeat the benefits if necessary to show that the pain of giving up the money is less than the pleasure of satisfying the need. The salesman must realize that price is relative and that while the prospect may agree that the price is fair for the value received, he may not be willing to pay it. He may prefer to take fewer advantages and use the additional money to buy satisfactions of other needs.

7. **Should I buy?** This is the final decision in the sale. The salesman must emphasize the advantages and pleasures which start with the purchase of the product by contrasting them with the disadvantages of delay and missed enjoyment. Involved in the decision is the question "When should I buy?", and the salesman works toward convincing the prospect that he ought to start experiencing the benefits immediately. If the sale cannot be completed immediately, but the prospect is

otherwise "sold," the salesman asks for a date for completion and carefully follows up on it.

Putting the Sales Plan Together

We will study the various stages of the sale more intimately later and discuss some techniques successful salesmen use to lead the prospect to make the right decisions for a sale. But meanwhile, let's consolidate the planning outlines. Here (opposite page) is how they might appear on a common chart:

THE SELLING FORMULA

Stages in the Sale	Prospect's Mental Steps	Prospect Decisions
1. PROSPECTING Salesman finds and qualifies prospects		
2. PRE-APPROACH Salesman studies prospect, plans presentation		
3. APPROACH Salesman gets interview, meets prospect	Attention Interest	Shall I see him? Shall I listen?
4. DEMONSTRATION Salesman uncovers needs, shows features, advantages, benefits	Interest Desire Conviction	Shall I listen? Do I need the benefits? Does his product give them? Is this the best source? Is the price right?
5 OBJECTIONS Salesman probes for objections, meets them, re-sells benefits	Desire Conviction	
6. CLOSING Salesman leads prospect to decision to buy now or accept proposal	Action	Should I buy? When should I buy?

Finding and Qualifying Prospects

I F YOU are not satisfied with the number of sales you are making, there is only one reason. You aren't seeing enough of the RIGHT kind of prospects in the RIGHT way.

Pretty rough analysis, isn't it? But examine it more closely. Every sale you make comes about because you found a certain prospect who was ready to buy when you saw him, or who was ready to buy after you explained your proposition. Right? The timing, your presentation, and the prospect were just right. When you gave the *same* presentation to many other prospects, they *didn't* buy. What was the difference between your *successful* sales efforts and the *unsuccessful* ones?

Sure, competition, products and price enter the picture, but the *main difference* is that when you made the sale, you told your story to the *right* prospect at the right time.

Every Sale Starts with a Prospect

The first stage every salesman must go through to complete any sale is prospecting. He must first find and qualify prospects who can use and pay for his product. This may take just a few seconds as with the peddler on the street corner, or it may take hours of searching through directories and making telephone calls.

The product and the market obviously affect the problem of finding prospects. If the product has a very restricted use, say in atomic energy plants, finding prospects is a minor problem. When everyone uses the product, life insurance for example, the problem becomes one of finding the *qualified* prospect to avoid wasting time and energy. With salesmen of necessities, the prospecting problem is different from that of a salesman selling luxuries. The same is true with industrial salesmen as opposed to consumer salesmen. But *every* salesman must develop his ability to find and qualify prospects for both his immediate and his future success. It has been estimated that this skill accounts for 80% of the success in some lines of outside selling.

Prospects Insure the Future

If you have a fine list of customers now and servicing and selling them takes most of your time, do you need to prospect? You do if you plan on making selling your career and you hope to move up progressively to the higher income levels.

Every salesman can name customers who were once big buyers but are not too important now, just as he can name customers who are important now but weren't much when first contacted. Good customers are lost for various reasons. They move, they have a change in management, they switch to a competitor, they no longer need your products or service. This endless turnover demonstrates that you keep building a good list of qualified prospects to replace the losses and to expand your list of the better quality customers.

Where to Find Prospects

Studies made on the salesman's problem with prospects boil down to these brutal revelations of the deficiencies in the poorer salesman that keep him from finding and qualifying enough good prospects:

1. He doesn't know they exist.
2. He doesn't know where to find them.
3. He is too lazy to look for them.

We will ignore the third reason because there's not much we can do about it here. But let's consider the other two.

Every salesman, even the best ones, pass by good prospects every day without recognizing them. A new company comes to town. A small company grows and needs the salesman's products now but didn't when he previously contacted them. A change in management makes the company more receptive to the salesman's offer. Existing customers now have additional needs that could be filled by the salesman if he were aware of this developing potential.

Every salesman will miss these prospect opportunities to some degree, but the better salesman will take nothing for granted, will do more checking, more prodding, more observing to catch them.

11 Sources for Prospects

1. **Present Customers.** Customers are naturally the source of re-orders. But present customers are also *prospects* for the goods and services you are *not now selling them!* Many a salesman remembers with regret how, in the course of a routine call on a good customer, he learned that the customer had bought something from a competitor. When asked about it, the customer replied, "Oh, I didn't know you sold it, too. I would have been glad to buy it from you."

Experienced salesmen make it a point to show the old customer new items on every call. Some use a part of their call record card to check the products that have been demonstrated to each customer. Those not yet checked are scheduled for future calls. This plan eliminates the chance of the customer not being aware of your full line. Just for fun, run a check on a dozen good customers and make a list of what they are NOT buying from you now. Chances are you will find twelve good prospects right there!

To be on the safe side, treat every customer as a good prospect for those items they are not buying from you *now.* They are the best kind of prospects. They are easier to sell than a new account. They are already sold on you and your firm.

2. **The Endless Chain.** Successful salesmen use their present satisfied

customers to forge an endless chain of prospects. Customers are flattered when you ask them for the names of friends who might be in the market for your product or service. The request for prospects is particularly timely just after you have completed a sale and the customer is pleased and in an agreeable mood.

The endless chain method of finding prospects works like the familiar chain letter. Suppose you start with one of your present customers and get enough leads to end up with two more customers. You get leads from these and end up with four more customers. Repeating the process with equal success just fifteen times would add 32,000 customers from prospects started with just one customer! Of course, like the usual chain letter, the system doesn't work perfectly. But would you settle for just 3,200 new customers? Or 320? How about 32? However it comes out for you, the Endless Chain technique will be well worth trying. Ask your customers for prospect leads and referrals. Ask permission to use their names.

3. **Inactive Customers.** How would your sales volume be if you had all your past customers back on your list? Make a list of your inactive accounts. Weed out the impossible ones. Consider the rest as prospects. Find out why they quit buying and see if you can get them restarted. There may have been some changes since you last saw them that will make a big difference.

4. **Similar Businesses.** If you sell to business firms, use the sale to one type of business as a testimonial wedge to sell the same thing to similar business. If the sale made one lawyer happy, it could make other lawyers happy. If the sale made a garage operate more efficiently, it will make other garages do so, too. Use directories to find allied businesses. Prospects will welcome the chance to hear you describe what another firm is doing.

5. **Advertising.** The firm behind the salesman usually invests a considerable amount of money in advertising to get prospects. But unless every lead the advertising produces is followed up quickly by the salesmen, the advertising is wasted. The prospect is attracted by the advertising and is interested in the product. Unless you get there while he is hot, a competitor could capitalize on the advertising success just because he happened to drop in at the right time.

6. **Centers of Influence.** This is a term used in selling circles for persons whose particular position gives them influence over other people as well as information that can enable the salesman to identify good pros-

pects. Business executives, teachers, bankers, politicians and building managers are examples. The center of influence, when he is helpful to the salesman, goes beyond the simple referral. He may make appointments, recommend the salesman or his proposition. The center may offer his influence out of pure friendship or he may expect favors in return. The least he expects is to be kept informed and to be appreciated. The smart salesman does these things.

7. **Bird Dogs.** Sometimes these are called "junior salesmen" or spotters. They keep a lookout for prospects for the salesman, frequently get a reward from the salesman if he makes the sale as a result of their tip. Route men, service and repair men, other people whose jobs involve meeting the public, make good spotters.

8. **Newspapers.** News stories give many leads to the salesman who reads them with this in mind. Weddings, obituaries and real estate transactions are favorite prospecting events for salesmen with products or services related to the persons involved. Salesmen who sell to the industrial market watch for items on new businesses, reorganizations, staff promotions, new branches, expanded production, big contracts awarded, new owners, moves to a new location. The approach method is to congratulate the prospect on the good news, then offer the services. If the news is bad, the offer is to help solve the resulting problems.

9. **Directories and Published Lists.** There are a number of directories that are full of prospects. Undoubtedly the classified telephone directory is the most used. While owning a telephone is only a slightly selective factor, and tells nothing about the actual quality of the prospect, the directory does a great time-saving job in breaking the firms down by types of business.

Libraries, chambers of commerce or boards of trade have other directories that will be helpful in the search for specific types of prospects. These include the city directories, Dun and Bradstreet, the state industrial directories, Thomas's Register of Manufacturers, and Poor's Directory of Directors.

Mailing list concerns compile special lists of individuals and firms for mail advertisers, but these can also be used by salesmen for prospects. They are compiled from directories and other sources, and are brought up to date constantly. In using a directory or list, it is very important to check the correctness of the name and address. It is not unusual for lists to change 25% to 50% annually depending on the individual and occupation.

Membership directories of trade associations, civic clubs and social and professional societies are sources of buyers. Sometimes these are available from the organization headquarters, but more often they are available only from members.

Municipal, county, state and national records can be used by salesmen as a source of prospects in almost every line of business. The county assessor's list shows the address and assessed valuation of every property owner. Tax lists, building permits, voting registration lists, license lists, are just some of the sources that show names, addresses and other data on general or specific types of prospects.

Many non-competitive salesmen have had success in trading prospect and customer lists with other salesmen. Having the original salesman describe the prospect gives the new salesman a great advantage in preparing for the interview.

10. **Listening.** Be a good listener! Conversation with friends or acquaintances, or even plain eavesdropping, can give you prospect leads. You go to clubs and social gatherings. The people you meet there are potential prospects or represent prospect firms. You must use good taste and avoid open solicitation, of course, and you must be careful not to betray a confidence. But with tact and diplomacy, you can make good use of your listening habits.

11. **Canvassing.** The straight canvass is not last on this list because it is least important. On the contrary, it produces leads which cannot be uncovered in any other way. For some types of selling, it is the primary source of sales.

Every salesman will agree that canvassing is a tough way to get leads, but you will also find the least competition there. Intelligent, selective canvassing can produce a high rate of returns. Knocking on every door may not be as profitable as following up selected leads, but when the prospect list starts to get low, you will find there are few substitutes for "pounding the pavement."

4 Ways to Qualify the Prospect

No matter how good a salesman you are, you can't sell a good order to a poor prospect! Even if you could sell a big order to some prospect, perhaps you shouldn't. How can you tell whether or not a prospect will make a good customer? Only by *checking him out!*

1. **What is his potential?** A prospect individual or firm has a certain

potential for using the salesman's product. The potential of course can be so low that it would be a waste of time to call on the prospect when there are others with more promising potential. How to evaluate the prospect? The indicated income of the individual, and the size of a business firm are *outward signs* of sales potential. So these are taken into consideration for the first screening. We know that this is not the *only* criterion. People whose outward signs say that they can't afford luxury automobiles sometimes buy them anyway. Pending further screening — with the help of such aids as Dun & Bradstreet, industrial directories, chambers of commerce, associations, credit bureaus, annual reports, suppliers, etc. — the salesman plays the averages, and he directs his attention *first* to those prospects who show the most likely potential and then to those whose worth is less obvious.

2. **What are his needs?** A person or firm may be able to buy the salesman's product but have no need for it. That takes them off the good prospect list. For things that everyone needs, like food, everyone is a prospect. When this is the case, some other criterion must be used. But as a rule, the salesman can quickly qualify his prospects by their need for his product. He may do this as he checks his prospect sources, or as he walks into the home or office. Or he may do it in his Approach, through a few leading questions.

3. **Can he buy?** In a typical firm, there is only one person with the authority to buy your product, the purchasing agent, a department head, the boss himself. In a home, it may be the husband or it could be the wife. Whoever it is, your job is to get to him quickly or you will waste your time talking to the wrong people.

Don't overlook the fact, however, that other people — the secretary, the wife, the kids — can *influence* the person who can sign the order. But you still need to know whom you must finally satisfy . . . who can buy?

4. **Can he pay?** No matter how good the salesman is, or how eager the prospect is to buy, all the energy is wasted if the prospect can't pay for what he does buy. Unless the salesman can work out some manner of payment, there is no sense in going through the effort of selling the prospect.

Where possible, credit information should be studied carefully before contact is made to determine if it warrants a sale. If the salesman doesn't know the credit history, he had better go cautiously, particularly if the prospect seems quite anxious to buy!

Prospects Protect Your Future

The salesman must constantly look for prospects or he will fail. The good customers of today, no matter how satisfactory the sales volume they give the salesman, may be lost tomorrow for one reason or another. The salesman must replace them or suffer a drop in income. The same holds true if the salesman believes that he has not yet reached the top of his potential, his earning power. The needed additional sales must come either from existing customers or from new prospects that convert to new customers. Through prospecting, qualification and cultivation, the salesman assures his future success.

Getting the Sales Interview

Y OU can get an interview with *anyone* in the world. Just get someone to make an appointment for you! This is one of the 10 keys for getting the interview with the one person who has the authority to buy the products or services you sell.

Sales managers used to pay their salesmen on the basis of the number of calls they made. As a result, salesmen would rush from door to door shouting, "Can I sell you anything today?" One salesman almost made a record of 100 calls in a single day. And he would have made it easily, but one prospect insisted on placing an order.

Now we know that just making calls is not enough. Sure, you will make more sales if you make more calls. The law of averages insures that. But if it's higher volume and not just numbers of sales you're after, then you need something more.

Today, the selling technique for creating higher profit sales is to first find out who has the authority to authorize the purchase, and then to arrange for an interview with that person.

Almost anyone in a company, including the elevator operator, can tell you with authority, "No, we don't need any of your merchandise today." But there are only one or two people in the typical firm who have the right to say yes. "Yes, I'll listen to your story, and if you convince me, I can authorize the purchase of your product." That's the person you want to interview.

Anyone can see the man who is easy to see. Usually he is easy to see because he doesn't have the responsibility of making the buying decision. He may be a subordinate with authority to say nothing but no. Or he may be a fellow who has already been sold, or doesn't have the money to buy. Or he may be a really tough character whose technique for handling salesmen consists of the quick interview and abrupt turndown.

On the other hand, the hard-to-see men — the Mr. Bigs among your prospects — are not only much more profitable to you in terms of time and sales but they are better prospects for a reason other than their position and authority as company buyers. The fact that they are hard to see means that you face less competition from other salesmen when you try for an interview with them than you do when trying to see subordinates. Let's see how the professional salesman gets in to see him.

The Castle Guards

If important executives — the ones you are aiming at — saw every salesman who wanted to see them, they would have little time for anything else. So they are forced to build themselves a sheltered fortress manned by tough, skilled guards called "secretaries" or "receptionists."

Salesmen must expect the secretary-receptionist to ask, "What do you wish to see Mr. Big about?" It's her job to keep her boss from wasting his time. But it is also her job in the screening process to let those people through who can *benefit* the boss or the firm. Sometimes it pays to give part of your presentation to the private secretary to convince her that the benefits are there. For example: "We just finished a survey of several plants similar to this one and we came upon several procedures for saving time and expense which might work here. Mr. Big could tell if they would or not if I could explain them to him."

Be careful with the truth. Seldom will a salesman have something to say to Mr. Big that is personal, confidential or greatly important. You might be able to fool the secretary and Mr. Big enough to get in on this basis once, but the chances of making a sale as a result will suffer.

Be courteous, tactful, polite and considerate with the receptionist, but don't take a "no" too easily. Be a little deaf to the first refusals, and keeping on selling the interview.

If you expect to make more than one call, be careful to show appreciation for any assistance. Remember the names of the persons you contact. Make each one feel important. Your continued success depends on it.

If the "guard" insists that Mr. Big is too busy, or is tied up, and it is impossible to see him now, make a definite appointment for another time. If the schedule is tight, try asking for an odd time, like 11:20 a.m., instead of 11 or 11:30. The chances are remote that this peculiar time has been specifically reserved. This will only work, of course, if you think that ten minutes will be enough to get the prospect sufficiently interested to go into the matter further at another time.

There Is No A-E-D

If there existed such a thing as an Automatic Executive Door-Opener, we'd all be out making fortunes in selling. Unfortunately, there is none. If there were a single golden key that could open most executive doors, however, it would probably be this: "Prove to the prospect or his guards that you are able to provide a real service to the executive or his firm." Unless you can do this, you don't deserve to get in.

10 Keys to the Executive Sanctum

Here are 10 keys successful salesmen all over the world use singly or collectively to get into the presence of the executive who can listen to their sales proposition and take the action that leads to profitable sales. Try them yourself!

Key No. 1. Expect to get in. You must first feel wholeheartedly that you have a right to the interview. You get this feeling by knowing your products and what they will do and by knowing your prospect and his firm and what they need.

Dress as if you expected to get in. Suffice it to say that if you dress like a bum, you'll probably be treated like one.

Talk like you expected to get in. Don't talk like a beggar or peddler. Don't say, "May I see Mr. Walters?" It only invites questions. Simply say, "Will you please tell Mr. Walters that Mr. Smith is here?"

Act as if you expected to get in. Don't grovel your way in. Walk in briskly and state your mission. If you have to wait, do it with an air of expectation, not as though you were settling down for the weekend. Some salesmen make it a point to wait no longer than 15 minutes except in unusual circumstances. At the end of that time, they tell the receptionist, "I must leave in a moment for another appointment." The receptionist usually tries to get the salesman in. If unsuccessful, the salesman asks her to phone the executive's secretary for him. He then asks the secretary, "Will you please see if Mr. Walters can see me at 3:15 on Thursday?" If this procedure doesn't produce an immediate audience, the salesman usually has a firm appointment for the next time.

Key No. 2. Ask for the interview. You may think this rule too simple to put down. Yet many salesmen fail to take the precaution of asking for the interview. Few executives will refuse to give you an interview at some future time no matter how busy they are today. There's real satisfaction when the receptionist looks at you coldly and asks, "Do you have an appointment?" and you can say sweetly, "Yes, I have".

Key No. 3. Use letters for introductions. Here are five ideas for using a letter to pave the way for an interview:

a. Send letter from the head of your company to the executive prospect.

b. Send letter saying, "Unless I hear from you, I will call at 2:45 next Wednesday." If he turns this down, at least you can make an appointment that suits him. If he doesn't answer, you can tell the guards, "Yes, I have an appointment."

c. A longhand letter seems to get more results than a typed form letter.

d. Send some literature with the letter, then call within a few days.

e. Even though the executive shunts you off to another person after he gets your letter, you then have his authority to talk the matter over with the lesser man.

Key No. 4. Forge an endless chain of introductions. This rule is simple enough. Just ask each customer in turn to give you an introduction to other prospects. Use his name (with his permission), or arrange for some other form of introduction. A phone call, a letter, or even his card will help you get past the guards.

Key No. 5. Use cards right — or not at all. Unless your company is big or important, go easy on the business card handouts. If your company is not well known, better use a card with only your name.

Key No. 6. Offer a service. We have said that you should have a right to get the interview because you have something the prospect needs. In getting the interview, stress this service rather than the merchandise you have for sale. Everyone buys *what a product will do,* not the product itself. Add your own service to what the product will do. Offer to study his present procedure, then give suggestions.

Key No. 7. Give something free. Don't pass up this means of getting inside the door. Fuller Brush salesmen have been getting in to see your wife for years by offering her a choice of some free brushes. It will work for you, too. The principle of the gift is to win your prospect's favor by buying his time. The gift need not be tangible. But it must have value to the prospect — a suggestion for increasing his profits, an idea for getting more business, a way toward greater progress.

Remember, the gift is not going to make the sale for you. It merely opens the door.

Key No. 8. Make a small request. Let's face it. Businessmen hate to waste time on salesmen. So think up a small request that is easy for them to fulfill.

Some salesmen ask, "Will you let me have just three minutes to explain an idea I have to reduce your letter-writing expense? If, at the end of that time, you are not interested, I'll leave." You might use something like: "I want to show you a picture of the new Acme installation," or: "I have a survey report here that I think you would like to see."

Key No. 9. Ask a favor. Did you ever realize that you feel more important when someone asks you to do them a favor? Except, possibly, when they want to borrow five dollars. Benjamin Franklin in his autobiography tells how he made fast friends with an opposition member of the General Assembly who had made a speech against his appointment. Franklin simply asked him the favor of reading a very scarce book the man had in his library. Franklin then quoted the maxim, "He that has once done you a kindness will be more ready to do you another than he whom you, yourself, have obliged.

You will find that the prospect who likes to turn down salesmen will seldom refuse to grant a favor, especially if he feels important in granting it.

There's no limit to the kind of favors you can ask — to speak at your club; to let you see some installation at his firm; to tell a friend of yours how he runs his training program.

Key No. 10. Make friends in the firm. Don't underestimate the power of *any* person in the firm. Don't take chances by offending any of them.

Next week one of them might be the Mr. Big you are trying to sell! Treat everyone you contact with courtesy and respect. Many of the lesser lights have influence on the brighter ones that can mean success or failure as far as your sale is concerned.

These ten keys will help you get interviews with men who have the authority to buy and pay for your product. Don't waste time on those who can only tell you, "No, we don't need any today." Start planning your attacks on the fortresses of the important men today. You'll find that the door opens easily once you use the right key. And you'll find Mr. Big is usually Good Joe once you convince him that you have something he can use — profitably.

Approaching the Prospect

W HAT happens in the *first 30 seconds* of the sales interview can be more important than anything you say or do in the next *thirty minutes!* In fact, if the start isn't right, you may not get a chance to stay around for *three minutes!*

While experienced salesmen will not agree on exactly what should take place within the first few minutes in the prospect's presence, they do agree on the importance of this short span of time. So much so, in fact, that it has its own identification in the outline for making a sale — the Approach.

Some authorities consider the problems and techniques involved in getting the interview as part of the approach, some prefer to classify it as part of the pre-approach. It matters little what you call it, as long as you handle it properly.

Now you will meet your prospect face to face, possibly for the first time. Now the vital moments are about to start.

What Is Your Objective?

Packed into the few minutes of the approach to the sales interview are two important objectives: (1) To gain the favorable attention of the prospect, and (2) to develop this attention into positive interest. These are accomplished through your appearance, your actions, and what you say — all equally important in these first critical moments.

The *physical* approach to the customer is over in a few seconds. It is the easiest for the salesman to accomplish, yet so many misjudge its importance and fluff it off. In the first few seconds, the prospect makes two very important decisions — (1) "Shall I SEE this guy?" and (2) "Shall I LISTEN to him?"

The answers to these questions by the prospect determine whether or not the rest of your presentation stands a chance.

That Important First Impression

The prospect's first impression of the salesman is a *visual* one. If he is favorably impressed, he is more likely to want to listen to you. If he is not, everything you say or do must overcome a serious handicap to succeed. If you look and act like a rude and careless person, you'll be treated like one.

Appearance is the total of many things. It is taste, cleanliness, attitude and general self-respect. It seems trite to tell a salesman that he must be clean and well-groomed, and yet many try to succeed without paying sufficient attention to these details. Why gamble away the chance for a sale on such easily corrected prospect distractions as rumpled and soiled clothing, unshined shoes, dirty fingernails, unshaved face, mussed hair?

The salesman's *attitude* should be a balance between confidence and conceit. He must show confidence in his merchandise, in his firm and in himself. Any lack of this confidence as revealed by his manner, his facial expression and his speech is quickly telegraphed to the mind of the prospect. Confidence must not be carried to the extreme of conceit, boastfulness or egotism, of course.

11 Suggestions for Favorable First Impressions

Before we discuss several techniques for developing a good Approach, here are some suggestions for general appearance and conduct.

1. Be neat in dress. Wear clothes on the conservative side.

2. Be clean in dress and body.

3. Maintain a confident bearing and manner — not superior, nor inferior, either.

4. Talk with a "smile," with a pleasant rather than a sour tone.

5. Have the name correct and pronounce it properly. Check with someone if necessary.

6. Leave wraps outside if possible. They detract if carried or held.

7. Do not intimate that the call is unimportant or casual, that you "just happened to be passing by."

8. Do not apologize for taking the prospect's time.

9. Handshake? A good rule is: let the prospect decide. No bone-crushers or limp-fish shakes in any case.

10. Sit down if possible. If the prospect doesn't offer a chair, ask, "May I sit down?"

11. Do not smoke. Your cigarette detracts in many ways from your presentation even where it doesn't antagonize the prospect. Is it worth waiting a few more minutes for the smoke to get the sale? If the prospect invites you to join him, use your own judgment. But put the cigarette down, safely in a tray, while you do your presentation.

We have said that the first objective of the approach is to get the prospect's *favorable* attention. Anyone can gain attention with sarcasm, crude stunts, or insults, but it is not *favorable* attention. You may read stories of salesmen landing sales with these tactics, but what you won't read about are the thousands that are lost in the same way.

13 Techniques for a Successful Approach

Here are some suggestions from successful salesmen for getting the favorable attention of the prospect and stimulating his interest in hearing more about your proposition. You will not be able to use all of the suggestions in any one sale, of course. Choose the ones most appropriate.

1. **Identify the purpose of the call first.** The typical salesman starts the approach with something like this: "Good morning, Mr. Riley. I'm

Jack Foster of Acme Products Co." Now, if the first ten seconds in front of the customer are the most important, Jack Foster is wasting them by greeting the prospect with the least interesting of pertinent facts. If he truly appreciates the importance of getting attention quickly, he will say instead, "Mr. Riley, I want to show you an idea that may help you reduce your costs. I'm Jack Foster of Acme Products Co."

2. **Ask a question that leads into the prospect's interest.** Questions are handy tools, but some of them used for openings are pretty worthless, like "Isn't this a beautiful day?", or "Well how's business?". The latter could ruin the whole show if business was bad — unless you could do something to improve it! The *right* questions will make the prospect think about the needs he wants to satisfy. In place of the pleasant irrelevancy or the routine question, ask: "Would it interest you to learn how you can shorten the time of handling outgoing shipments?"

3. **Get the prospect to participate.** A person can pretend to listen, but he just can't continue with one line of thought and actively participate in another. So the salesman gets the prospect into the act by involving one or more of his senses. "Hold that." . . . "Feel this." . . . "How do you like this smell?" . . . "Just look under the flap?" . . . "Look at this." . . ."Push this down."

4. **Promise a benefit.** "I think I have an idea that will save you money." What can a prospect say except "How?" or "Prove it." Offering the benefit in the form of a question is a tested technique for getting quick results: "Mr. Hall, if I could show you how to save 15% on your car rentals, would you be interested?" You can combine this technique with technique. No. 1, asking a question about a benefit before you identify yourself or at least before mentioning your firm.

5. **Offer a survey.** "Mr. Parker, I have a product that may be able to reduce your maintenance costs, but I'm not sure. With your permission, I'd like to check a few things about your operation first and report back to you." The prospect will usually respond by asking more questions about the product.

6. **Offer a trial.** The trial is more frequently used later in the sales interview when an immediate sale cannot be made, but it can also be suggested in the approach. "Mr. Gardner, we have just received a new stapler with an anti-jamming device. We would like to have you try it out for a few days and see if it can speed up your bagging operation."

7. **Open with the product.** If your product can stimulate interest just

by its appearance, it alone can be used for the opener. Salesmen use this approach by walking in with the product in their hands and depositing it on the desk of the prospect. They may step back without saying a word. If the prospect is reasonably familiar with similar products, the salesman may give a simple comment, like: "Isn't that a dandy?" or: "Turn this switch." If there is some element of mystery about it, exploit it. "What do you think this is?" This approach can be combined with getting the prospect into the act by inviting him to taste it, smell it, feel it, listen to it, look through it, etc.

8. **Use a visual.** Instead of the actual product, visuals can be used. They can also be used to supplement the actual product, or they can demonstrate the services you are selling. A wide variety of visuals and audio-visuals are used — photos, models, cut-aways, charts, posters, slides, movies, tapes, etc. The salesman simply asks permission to show them. "Mr. Fellows, I would like to show you three photos taken of a welding operation using a new process. May I?" "I have a five-minute color film showing a new idea in displaying merchandise that I think would interest you. May I set the unit here? Where is the nearest outlet?"

9. **The shock treatment.** Open with a startling fact or a strong statistic. "Do you realize that you could actually save money by carpeting your general office instead of using the present flooring?" Obviously you must be able to back up your statement.

10. **Tell a story.** We all like to hear a story, provided it's stimulating and told well. The story can be combined with any of the other approaches we have mentioned. For example, the salesman can produce a shattered pair of safety glasses and, for a "shocker" approach, say, "These glasses cost a firm like yours $59,000." Then he can say, "Let me tell you what happened."

11. **Use a referral.** Use the name of another person as an introduction. "I believe you know Mr. Johnson of the Allied Company. He suggested that you would be interested in hearing what they are doing about . . ."

12. **Give him something.** Giving the prospect something of value can be used as an opener. It has worked for many years for the door-to-door brush salesmen. But it should direct the prospect's attention toward the product or service, and not itself alone. A free ballpoint pen or a thermometer are nice gifts, but the salesman must relate them to what he does next to stimulate interest. Otherwise, the prospect begins thinking about using the pen or thermometer and doesn't listen to what the sales-

man is saying. He might say, "I'd like to give you this new pen with our compliments. On the side you notice the words '24-hour service' . . ."

13. **Use a gimmick.** Here we can identify the thousands of stunts or gimmicks salesmen have used or will devise to get the prospects' attention. While they are planned to lead into the reason for the sales interview, they are strictly for attention. A salesman lights a match to what looks like a dollar bill. Another rolls a pair of dice on the prospect's desk. In using any stunt, remember the purpose must be to get *favorable* attention. And after getting attention, you must move quickly into stimulating the prospects' interest in satisfying a want.

We have covered several techniques for getting the prospect's favorable attention quickly and opening the way for you to capitalize on his interest. Think about what *you* usually say and do in those important first 30 seconds in the prospect's presence. Can your approach be improved? Get your first words and actions organized ahead of the call and you have increased your chances for carrying through a successful sales interview.

Making the Demonstration

PICTURES and words are fine, but demonstrations *make more sales!* The demonstration is the core of the third phase of the sale, the Presentation. The approach has been made, the prospect and the salesman are on the same wave length, and now the prospect settles back to listen to the salesman tell his story.

Repeated practice on a good demonstration assures the best possible technique. Once you have mastered a demonstration plan that produces results, do not change it unless you are convinced that revision will increase results. Do not change your technique simply because you are tired of the "old routine." It may cost you plenty in lost sales. Think of all the prospects who haven't seen your demonstration yet.

Many manufacturers spend considerable time and money perfecting effective demonstration techniques. Salesmen fortunate enough to get such help should take advantage of all the research involved and give the demonstration a real trial.

4 Steps to Successful Demonstrations

A full demonstration is simply the sum total of several small demonstrations that focus on simple steps or features. Master each small demonstration and you can't miss on the complete one.

A demonstration is composed of only four basic steps:

1. You say something.
2. You do something.
3. You get the prospect into the act.
4. You ask leading questions.

Step 1. Say something. What you say and how you say it throughout the demonstration can make or break the sale. These hints from the experiences of successful salesmen will help you improve your sales talk.

Be enthusiastic. Think back on your own shopping experiences. How did you react to the salesman who seemed just lukewarm about making a sale to you? Did he impress you favorably — like that other salesman, who met your inquiry with courteous attention and a wholehearted selling effort?

Use a conversational tone. Talk to your prospect like a friend. Don't act as if you're making a speech. Try to draw him into the conversation. What he says will help you find his interest and use it to make the sale. It may also bring to light and enable you to clear up any misunderstandings he may have about your product.

Talk slowly. Don't blanket your prospect with words. As we become more familiar with a product, we are apt to talk about it at a pace that outdistances the prospect's understanding. With our complete grasp of the story, we may even leave out details which seem insignificant to us but which might be the key to his appreciation of the product.

Take it easy. Assume the prospect knows nothing about your product until you are convinced otherwise. Talk slowly. Key your words with your actions.

Tell and show. Prepare your prospect for your demonstration so that he will focus his attention on the points you bring out. "I am going to show you how easy it is to make a tape recording with this machine. I take this sensitive microphone that comes with the machine and plug it in, like this." Funnel the prospect's attention on what you are going to do and what you are doing.

Step 2. Do something. There are four points to keep in mind as you go through the actions involved in your demonstration:

1. Put the prospect's attention where you want it.
2. Take your time.
3. Make it look easy.
4. Don't fumble.

A simple device for getting the prospect's attention is to have him do something — move a lever, hold a paper, turn a crank. If there is nothing for him to do, simply say, "Look at this," or, "Watch what happens when I push this lever."

Don't rush your demonstration. Those points which you omit, or which whiz by the prospect because you are in too big a hurry, might be the very ones that would clinch the sale!

After you get familiar with a demonstration you will become so good at it that you can speed it up considerably. But don't do it! Keep your pace down to where the prospect can follow you. Ask questions, repeat if necessary, review those features which are particularly important to the prospect.

After you have given your demonstration several times, you may get the same feeling you have when you see a movie for the third time. Don't forget, though, that this is a first run for your prospect. Don't let repetition dull your delivery.

Make it look easy. If you are stressing your product's simplicity of operation, it is important that whatever you demonstrate looks easy to do.

Practice each element of your demonstration until you can do it smoothly and easily. The prospect assumes that you are an expert. If you, the expert, can't operate the machine, what chance has a novice?

Part of making it look easy is to avoid fumbling, a distraction that shatters the prospect's concentration on the point you are developing. Some fumbling comes from lack of experience. Practice can cure this. But another variety of fumbling comes from lack of planning — looking for this, losing that, dropping something that was out of place. A carefully planned demonstration is the best cure for fumbleitis."

Step 3. Get the prospect into the act. When your prospect participates in the demonstration, you are assured of his attention. You give him the feeling of operating his own machine. You increase the chances of his retaining the selling features you present.

Successful salesmen take these steps to promote prospect participation:

1. Have him do something simple.
2. Have him work an exclusive feature.
3. Have him do something he would do often if he had the product.

You want the prospect to be able to do the thing you ask easily and without embarrassment. Stay away from the complicated jobs.

Part of the value of getting the prospect into the act is to help him remember your product's superior features. Make a list of the features, then select the ones that can be used for emphasis when the prospect takes part in the demonstration.

Your prospect may already be using another type of product similar to yours. He may have shopped around and tried out competitive equipment. If you get him to do something in the demonstration which he would do often if he owned the product, he has a better chance of "seeing" how much time he would save, how much simpler the operation is, or the advantages you have to offer.

Step 4. Ask leading questions. Questions are valuable tools in making sales. They get the customer to make a commitment so you can check on the progress of your demonstrations. Questions help you find out the prospect's interest so you can select and emphasize the product features which best fit those interests. Questions flatter the prospect, for we all like to give others our opinions.

Use questions:

1. To check the effectiveness of your demonstration.
2. To move your demonstration along.
3. To get the prospect into an agreeable mood.

After you have made a point in your presentation, ask a question to determine whether or not it was understood. If the answer shows that it was, go on with your next feature.

Questions should be worded so that:

1. They call for an *affirmative* answer, or
2. They call for a *longer* answer.

Compare these two questions: "This is really easy to operate, isn't it?" "This isn't hard to operate, is it?" Are they the same? In thought, perhaps, but the first one is much better for selling purposes! It is called an affirmative question because it calls for a "yes" answer.

As you progress with your questioning, it is much better to have the prospect nodding yes, yes, yes, than shaking his head no, no, no. When you get to the point of asking for his order, you want him to be in the mood to continue to say yes.

Questions can be used to set the stage for closing the sale. The question, "Do you feel that this new cleaner would save you time in floor maintenance?" makes the prospect mentally place the product in use by his cleaning crew, in his own building. When he agrees, he has committed himself to accepting the fact that your cleaner will save time.

Little questions lead to little agreements. Little agreements add up to one big agreement . . . your sale!

Overcoming
Objections

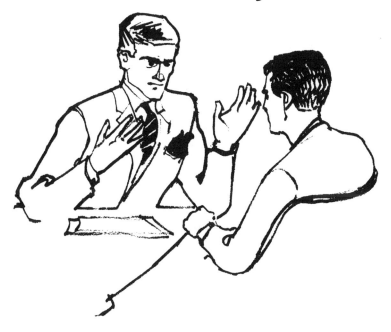

THE successful salesman welcomes objections. To the inexperienced salesman this may sound like a ridiculous statement. Welcome objections? Yes, because they give the salesman clues to planning the next step in the selling procedure. Frequently, they can even be turned into selling points or advantages.

The worst type of prospect is the one who sits back, listens attentively to your story, nods pleasantly, but doesn't raise any objections. He just doesn't buy. When the prospect raises objections, you have handles to grip, signposts to point the way to important selling points.

As a rule, it is impossible to avoid objections in selling. If there were no objections, there would be no need for salesmen. When you realize that objections are a normal part of selling, you can plan to use them to your advantage.

3 Steps to Overcoming Objections

There are three important steps to overcoming the objections you face day in and day out. One without the others loses much if not all of its power. Here they are:
1. Know the *answer* to the objections.
2. Know the *techniques* for applying it.
3. Know *when* to use the technique.

Before you can handle objections, you must know the answers! No amount of skill in techniques for overcoming objections can make up for a lack of information about your product.

There is no simpler method for being prepared with the answers than to write the common objections down, then thoughtfully work out the best possible answers to each one. Many sales managers conduct sales meetings for this purpose, asking the salesmen to contribute their most common objections and suggested answers. From these contributions each salesman builds his defense. Manufacturers, too, furnish their dealers with answers to common objections.

As you write out an answer to an objection, you're bound to get some technique mixed in with it. "I can understand why you don't want to spend money foolishly, Mr. Prospect (technique so far), but with this duplicator you can save time-consuming rewritings that cost much more than the low price of the machine."

9 Techniques for Overcoming Objections

Overcome objections with these successful techniques:

1. **Watch that temper!** If you're the least bit touchy, the prospect can set you off with an unreasonable objection. Letting him know how stupid, unfair, or untruthful he is may satisfy your urge, but it doesn't make sales. Regardless of how you feel under the collar, don't let your words, your voice, or your facial expression convey your feelings. Watch that smile, too. It's better to stay serious. Have you ever faced someone whose smile alone said, "Boy, you're a dumb so-and-so"?

2. **Listen attentively.** Let the prospect get the objection out of his

system. Don't cut him off with clever answers. As he hears himself talk, his objections sound less and less important. But if you jump right at it, he will defend his objections and magnify them. Just listen, don't interrupt.

3. **Don't argue—suggest.** Your position as a salesman is to cooperate with, not do battle with, your prospect. Few men and no women are convinced by an argument! By suggestions you lead them to come to their own conclusions. This could easily be a sales axiom: "Win an argument and lose a sale."

4. **Convert the objection into a question.** Questions invite answers, while objections only invite arguments. When you convert a prospect's objections into a question, you can answer it smoothly and kindly without proving he is wrong. But if you prove him wrong on his objection, you embarrass him and force him to uphold his stand.

Suppose the prospect says, "We can't afford to use your bearings." Instead of saying, "Oh yes, you can," say "You raise a wise question: Will the use of our bearings be an unnecessary expense? Is that the question?" If the answer is no, you can get to the real question. If it is yes, you can answer the question, showing how your bearings will actually save him money. End with: "Does that answer your *question*, Mr. Prospect?" Don't call it an *objection*.

Restate objections that may be vague. If this can be done by reforming the objection into a question, so much the better. By all means, do not exaggerate the objection.

5. **Handle the objection at once.** You will find situations where you would prefer to postpone the answers to objections. Price objections, petty objections, or objections whose answers are scheduled to be developed later in the interview, for example. But most successful salesmen say, "Meet the objection the moment it is raised." Here are some reasons behind this advice:

The prospect may keep thinking about the objection you say you will answer later. In the meantime, he may not be listening to what you are telling him. Or he may think you are groping for an answer and lose confidence in you. The particlar objection may be the only obstacle to the close. Handle it effectively and you speed up the sale.

The early price objection is common and it is natural to want to postpone the answer until you get through with your sales talk. When the objection is obviously a stall, you are justified in acknowledging it and postponing the answer until you have a chance to awaken desire for your product. Here are some examples of how that tactic can be employed. "Yes, that looks like a lot of money. But let's not consider price until we know which model you could use. Maybe you don't need one at all." If you have several models and prices, say in answer to a price question (which is a form of objection), "I can't give you a price until we find out just which model will suit your needs most. Maybe I can't help you at all."

"The price is $250. But let's just write that down here and forget it temporarily while we talk about your present method." In this latter example, you can write down savings figures opposite the price as you develop your presentation. These will minimize the price objection.

6. **Let references give the answer.** When you and your prospect talk, you may come to verbal blows that settle nothing. It's like the kids' arguments. Bringing in a neutral third party softens your answer. "I can understand how you feel, Mr. Prospect. Bill Jones over at Ace Company felt that this system couldn't improve his warehousing methods. Let me show you a letter he wrote us after using our system a year." Now Bill Jones is giving the answer to the objection.

7. **Find the real objection.** Many objections hide the real ones. "Price too high" usually means "My desire is too low," and the answer should offer reasons to buy rather than argument for the price. Recognize the objection that is just a stall. Until you reach the real objection, you cannot overcome it and complete the sale.

8. **Don't offend.** It's easy to rebut an objection in such a way that you offend the prospect. Without actually saying so, you can imply that he is pretty dumb, is lying, or doesn't know what he is talking about. So be particularly careful in phrasing your answers.

You can take the edge off your reply in several ways:

a. By taking the blame away. For example, "I am sorry that I failed to make the point clear," or "You're quite right in feeling that way now, but as I go along . . ."

b. By making a concession first. "You are quite right that the price seems high at first. But when you consider . . ." Or, "Normally, that would be quite correct. With this meter, however . . ."

c. By saying that others feel the same way. "I frequently hear the same thought, and I can see why. But . . ." Or, "Jack Boyd at United said the same thing at first. But let me show you a photo . . ."

d. By paying tribute to the idea. "I admire your stand, but . . ." Or, "I know you have the interests of your company at heart."

9. **Answer possible objections before they're raised.** After you have had experience selling any particular line, you are familiar with objections that are raised over and over again. The smart salesman forestalls these objections by incorporating the answers to them into his sales presentation. Don't expect to eliminate all objections this way, of course, but you will have smoother sailing to the close of the sale if you head off the more troublesome ones.

Recognize objections as a friend to help you close the sale, not an enemy to avoid. Be prepared with the answers, the techniques and the sense of timing that overcome both false and real objections and you will close more sales.

Closing the Sale

A WISE and successful industrial salesman once gave a group of new salesmen this advice: "Your sale isn't completed until you get the signed purchase order or ring the cash register." Nothing profound about that statement, you say? Certainly not, and yet a lot of selling action is wasted every day by salesmen who hesitate to make the final move that clinches the order.

Pleasant conversation is fine for keeping your prospects on friendly terms with your company. But closed sales give you lots more customers and commissions!

An automobile manufacturer once found in a survey that people liked the way some of his salesmen treated them in not forcing the sale. This was very gratifying until the manufacturer found that in every instance the person interviewed had bought a car from a competitor!

Have you ever been confronted with a salesman who made an excellent presentation, made you want his product, but then just stood there waiting for you to make the next move? He might have asked, "Are there any questions?" When you said, "No-o-o," half waiting for the order blank, he got to his feet, saying, "Well, if you ever do have any more questions, just feel free to call me and I'll be glad to answer them." Made you sort of feel like the girl who doesn't get kissed on the door step, yet you didn't feel it was your place to close the sale yourself.

You might laugh about such selling when you are the prospect, but it's tragic if you should happen to be the salesman. You can't feed your wife and kids just by answering questions.

Closing Need Not Be "High-Pressure"

High-pressure selling is old-style and frowned upon today. But there's nothing wrong with getting the customer to buy your goods by means of well-defined techniques for bringing the sale to a successful close.

Old-fashioned, high pressure methods were aimed at getting the order regardless of the prospect's needs or desires. Today's closing techniques are aimed at moving the prospect into making a decision after he is convinced that he wants the product.

Close from the Beginning

Making the sale is the sum total of the steps you go through from the time you first contact the prospect until he is satisfied with his purchase. All that you do during your selling interview is preparation for the act of closing.

Closing a sale has been likened to buttoning the last button on your overcoat. As the presentation progresses, you establish the features of your product and the benefits. As the prospect accepts each benefit, it is one more button buttoned. When the last button slips into its buttonhole, the sale is closed. If you have properly established the benefits, all you need to do is write up the order.

Ask a successful salesman for his one great rule in closing and you will usually hear: "Don't wait too long." More salesmen than we could ever count talk themselves out of a sale by prolonging it until the prospect tires, becomes resentful, or thinks up several more good reasons for not buying.

The early attempt to close may not work, but if it does, think of the time you save for other sales or for rounding up more prospects. Your only assets as a salesman is time, and every moment you spend needlessly because you don't close soon enough is a lost moment as far as your selling income is concerned.

6 Basic Ways to Close the Sale

We might be able to list 66 ways to close the sale, but the following six ways are basic and cover in principle many more specific methods used by individual salesmen.

1. **Trial Close.** Most salesmen call their first attempt to close a *trial close*. It is really more than a close. It is a check on how the prospect is responding. It usually takes the form of a question, like: "How many gallons do you think you would use in a month?" From the answers, you can tell whether or not you need to do more selling or if you are ready to go into the actual close.

Don't give up too soon! Use several trial closes until the prospect reacts properly. John Patterson, dean of sales trainers, told his National Cash Register salesmen to try for a close seven times before they turned in a report that a prospect couldn't be sold.

2. **Assumptive Close.** With this closing technique, the salesman merely takes for granted that the prospect is going to buy. It is used after a trial close or when the customer's reactions tell him that he is receptive to the product or proposition.

A common master word in the assumptive close is "when." "When do you have to have this delivered?" "How soon must you change these files?" If your prospect wants your product, there is a time when he wants it. By centering on the question of time, you require him to decide to buy without his being aware of any forcing.

There are other ways to use the assumptive close, of course. "From what you have told me, you will want the Model 23 Executive Desk. May I use this phone to see if we have it in stock?" If the prospect says you can use the phone, he, in effect, says that he will buy the desk. The principle of this close is to assume that the prospect will buy and to wrap up the minor details.

Fear prevents many salesmen from using this highly successful technique. Fear that the customer will say, "Hold everything! I didn't say I was going to buy." But what if he does? You then treat it as a trial close, find out what is stopping the prospect, and go on with the sale. If he doesn't object to the assumption, the sale is closed. What can you lose?

3. **"Which One" Close.** "Give him a choice" is a great rule of selling. It is also used as a closing technique. Although it is much like the trial close, it is used after you are more certain that the prospect is receptive

to your product. It is closer to the signing of the order. In fact, it may follow a trial close that has turned out right and become the actual clincher to the sale.

Common "whiches" are: which color? which size? which finish? which method of shipment? Your own order blank may require you to ask for information that will form the basis for the close: how many, model number, what size, where shipped, etc.

4. **Action Close.** A study of successful closers will show that they *do* as well as say something to bring about the close. At the right time they introduce a proposal to action that will close the sale automatically unless the prospect stops them. The technique is closely related to the assumptive close, but has action as the added feature.

The action close is not attempted until the prospect shows signs of being receptive. It is merely a tool for making up his mind to act, and you provide the tool.

Perhaps the most common action close consists of the writing of the order, then showing it to the prospect and asking, "Will you verify this *description?* I'll arrange to deliver it on the day you specify." Incidentally, "verify" seems to be better for closing than "sign here," or "O.K. this." Leave the word "order" out of it, too.

If the development of the sale involves a survey of present conditions related to the prospect's operation, his needs and solutions to those needs, the salesman can use the results of the survey for an action close. "Here's what we found you need, Mr. Jordan. If you will verify it, we can start saving you money by next Thursday." Of course, the list is written on an order blank, and his verification is his signature on the order.

This close is frequently expressed simply as: "Ask for the order." Many sales could have a happier ending if the salesman would only try to close. "That's the story. Shall we go ahead on that basis?"

5. **Inducement Close.** A number of closing techniques can be lumped under this heading. They offer an inducement to the prospect to buy right now rather than put it off. One important point about this close, however, is that it should be used only when others fail, when it's a matter of the inducement close or writing off the sale.

Offering an actual premium is a form of inducement, like free service on a machine for a year, a free storm door with an installation of storm windows, or a case of soap powder with a washing machine. We all like to get something for nothing.

Insurance against loss is another inducement to the sale. Many businessmen aren't particularly interested in making a few extra dollars, but they will fight hard to keep from losing the dollars they have. "Each day you operate without this system, Mr. Jackson, costs you $360. Let's start making the change immediately." "These towels were bought on a lucky purchase. When we get the new shipment we will have to charge more for them." "We have one table in stock with the exact finish you want. When that is sold, it takes about four weeks to get another one." "Next week our prices go up 10 per cent."

6. **Summary Close.** The summary is frequently combined with the action close. Here you say, "Now let me summarize what you get in this cleaning method." Some products lend themselves to a listing on a sheet of paper or an order blank. After the summary, you say, "There it is. If you will verify this list . . . ." Be brief with your summary by all means. Hit the features and benefits which appeared to you to make the greatest impression on the prospect.

That's Not All

There are naturally many more specific ways of closing the sale than we can mention here. But most of them will fall under one or more of these six categories. Certain products lend themselves to certain closing methods. Sometimes your own personality will allow you to use a closing technique which would not work for another salesman.

Determine now to make a conscious effort to close every sale, to close it as early as possible and to keep it closed with customer satisfaction. If you do, your future sales are bound to increase in number and value.

Selling
through
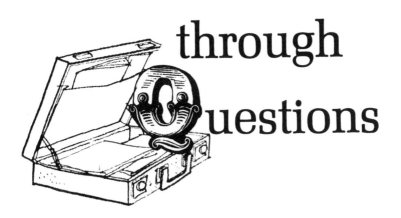
uestions

RUDYARD KIPLING may have had the salesman in mind when he wrote these words in 1902:

> *I keep six honest serving-men,*
> *(They taught me all I knew)*
> *Their names are What and Why and When*
> *And How and Where and Who.*

Questions are among the best tools in the salesman's selling kit. When handled skillfully, they bring the needs, the desires and the prejudices of the prospect out into the open so that the right decisions become obvious.

The inexperienced salesman tells and shows and tells some more until the customer withdraws, becomes unconcerned or even antagonistic. Skillful questioning, on the other hand, draws the prospect out and leads him into making the decision the salesman is after. When the prospect makes the decision himself, he is more convinced of its soundness and he is prepared to defend it. The salesman's proposal that he might have been inclined to challenge has now become his own decision to uphold.

Questions in the Approach

The question is a great device for getting the prospect's attention and interest during the approach. To answer the question, the prospect must break away from what he was doing or thinking about when the salesman appeared, and focus his attention on the salesman.

The opening question is usually developed from a study of the product you are selling or of the prospect's need which the product will solve.

The typical prospect will answer any reasonable question put to him in the proper manner. He does this out of habit or common courtesy. When the question involves a challenge, the interest develops in a hurry.

Many salesmen find that asking permission to ask further questions is a good approach because it puts the prospect on a pedestal, makes him feel important, and alerts him to field the questions. He can't think of other things while he is answering questions. The first question might be something like any of these:

"Mr. Prospect, do you mind if I ask you a few questions?"

"Mr. Prospect, I'm not sure that what I have to show you would be of help to you. May I ask a few questions?"

"Mr. Prospect, if I could show you how to cut the down time of your sewing machines, would you be interested?"

Of course the questions must be thoroughly designed to lead to the desired answers. A poor question can invite trouble. The typical opening questions of salesmen who haven't given the idea much thought are: "How's business?" or: "How do things look?". What can you do with answers to these questions if things are good? And you certainly get off to a bad start if the prospect is reminded that business is bad.

Fact-Finding Questions

Questions are used to qualify the prospect, to see if he is a good prospect for the salesman's goods and services. In some cases, the salesman finds a brief survey form helpful at this stage. Manufacturers and the home office frequently develop a list of questions or a survey form for the salesman based on past sales successes.

Fact-finding questions may be asked of the telephone operator, the receptionist, secretary, or any other member of the prospect firm during the pre-approach or qualifying period. But some of the questions, or all of them, may be directed to the prospect himself during the approach.

Salesmen find that they are seldom refused when they open the approach with, "Mr. Prospect, to be sure that I take a minimum amount of your time, do you mind if I first ask a few questions?" They then ask questions that establish the need for the salesman's product, or information about the buyer. For example:

"How many employees do you have?"

"Do you sell primarily to manufacturers, wholesalers or retailers?"

"Do you have your own floor maintenance crew or do you use an outside service?"

Questions to Get the Prospect's Opinion

Most products and services are offered as better solutions to specific problems, and the salesman's job is to tie these solutions to the prospect's matching problems. Getting the prospect to admit to the problems and then to discuss them is a goal that can be achieved through questions.

One form of questioning that has been used successfully by creative salesmen asks for the prospect's opinion on a situation involving a third party or parties. "A number of the office managers I call on tell me that the scarcity of floor space for adequate file storage is a growing problem. How do you feel about it?" When the prospect agrees that floor space is a problem, the salesman will obviously lead into a solution which his file cabinet or filing system offers.

Other question starters which lead to prospect opinions are: "Last week I read that . . ." "Mr. Gordon of the Wilshire Cleaners told me a few days ago that . . ." "A recent Department of Commerce report said that . . ." "Some of my customers have found that . . ."

After referring to the particular fact or situation, the salesman can hook it into the prospect's situation with any of these or similar questions: "Did this ever happen to you?" "What is your opinion on this?" "Do you think he had a good point?" "Do you consider this a problem?" "Has this ever concerned you?"

When the prospect has reacted to several questions, exposing his needs, desires or problems, the good salesman uses his responses as the opener for the solution and the sale. One way is to say, *"Based on what you have told me,* Mr. Prospect, it would seem that the solution would be . . ." If a third party can be brought in, so much the better. "Based on what you have told me, Mr. Prospect, would you like to hear what Bestfit Company did in a similar circumstance?"

Questions to Keep Prospect Talking

The salesman's immediate objective is to keep the prospect talking about his need and what he hopes to gain so that he will begin to accept the product or service as the best solution to that need. He can do this with questions and adroit reaction to the prospect's answers.

Psychologists say that we all respond to "reinforcement" and "rewards." We tend to keep doing something when we are rewarded for doing it. We tend to stop doing it when we are ignored or punished. The salesman rewards the prospect for his answers and keeps him talking by:

1. Praise for the action the prospect took.

2. Showing approval for the right answers, ignoring wrong ones.

3. Repeating the prospect's statement or key words.

The reward need not be great. In fact, a nod of the head, single word like "good," or an approving sound like "uh-huh" or even "hmmm," will be enough.

Questions to Check Prospect's Reaction

During the presentation, the salesman needs to find out if the story and proposal is getting through to the prospect. Does he understand the language? Is his attention or interest lagging? Is he accepting what you are saying? Is he still with you? If not, where did he leave? The answers to these questions are necessary cues for steering the presentation to final acceptance.

Obviously you cannot ask these questions as they are stated here. You can't ask, for example, "Is your attention lagging?" The questions must be skillfully worded and presented at the proper time to keep the prospect in step with the presentation. Here are some examples:

"How does that sound to you?"

"Would you like to have the same results?"

"Has this ever happened to you?"

"Would this appeal to your clients (or others affected by the idea)?"

"Do you agree with his statement?"

Write the questions into your sales presentation script at convenient spots. Word them as in the examples above, to fit the situation you have just described.

Questions to Probe Deeper

To get to the prospect's true motives or his real objections, the salesman needs to get a more telltale reaction than simple answers to his questions might provide. The questions designed to keep the prospect talking will bring more information from him, but there are times when we want to do more than to reward or reinforce. We may even want to antagonize to get more information on which to build the sale.

Here are typical questions for getting the prospect to tell you more after he has made a statement and stopped talking.

"Why do you say that?" — or just "why?"

"In what way?"

"Would you say the same thing if . . .?"

"Suppose I could lop off three minutes on each operation . . ."

Repeat a key word or phrase as a question and *wait* for more amplification:

"The colors faded?"

"What do you have in mind?"

"What do you think causes that?"

"Do you have any *other* reasons for feeling as you do?"

Questions to Assure Understanding

Communications is a difficult thing at times. When the salesman must know exactly what the prospect wants or objects to, he should ask questions for clarification. These may take the form of a restatement of the main points as they are understood. For example:

"Let me see if I understand." Repeat what the prospect said, then ask, "Do I have the right idea?"

"You are saying that if you could do the job with two welds you could save time and money. Right?"

Do not — repeat, DO NOT — imply by the wording of your question that the prospect just did a poor job of explaining or doesn't have a good command of the language. That's what openings like these would imply: "What you mean to say is . . ." "I don't follow you . . ." "Let me reword what you said." *You* can be stupid for not understanding, but don't make *him* look stupid.

People dislike to be "told" anything, but they don't mind getting answers to questions. By using the proper probing questions, the salesman draws the prospect's wants and desires into the open. These can then be formed into questions which need answering. The salesman says, "From what you have told me, it would seem that the question is, 'Can we reduce the cost of preparing the seals and at the same time retain their quality.' Do you agree?" If the prospect agrees that this is the question, then all the salesman has to do is answer the question and he is well on the way to the sale. If the prospect disagrees, then he himself rephrases the question and the salesman tries to answer it.

People dislike being "told" what to do, as we said, but they usually welcome suggestions. So the salesman phrases his remarks accordingly and "suggests" the right answers. "Based on what you have told me, do you mind if I make a *suggestion?*" The prospect can't refuse to listen to a *suggestion,* and he is more open-minded to it than he would be to a direct statement like: "You should install . . ."

The Salesman As Counselor

Salesmanship used to place the salesman in the center of the stage, making his "pitch" to his audience, the prospect. Now, thanks to research into sales motivation, the salesman is cast in the role of the counselor with the prospect as the center of attention. Instead of sitting back and listening to a presentation, the prospect now participates in an interview.

As in all interviews, the questions are the key to the quality of the responses. The successful salesman has mastered the art of using questions to induce the prospect to reveal his own needs, sharpen his own desires, form his own conclusions. The ultimate conclusion, of course, is to buy the salesman's product or proposition—NOW.

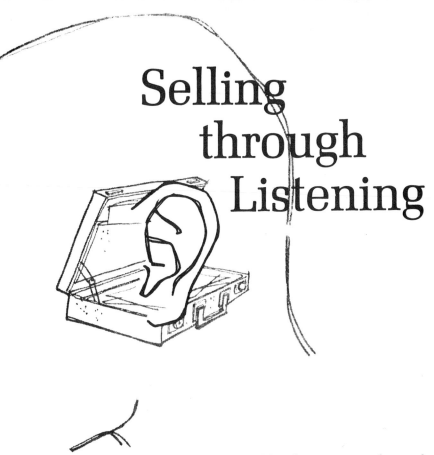

Selling
through
Listening

THE salesman would certainly be considered one person who needs to talk a lot to make a living. Yet studies show that he actually LISTENS more than he TALKS. And those experts who have studied the performance of salesmen tell us that most salesmen should do *even more listening* to their customers and less talking?

The typical salesman spends about 70% of his waking hours in communication with others. He is not unusual in this, because most people spend about the same proportion. Studies such as those made by the University of Minnesota show that the communications activity breaks down into about these proportions: 9% in writing; 16% in reading; 30% in talking; and 45% in listening.

The training we have received in schools is focused on the reading, writing and speaking phases of our communication problem. Yet we get little help in what is apparently the most time consuming area, listening! If 45% of a salesman's selling time is devoted to listening, then he ought to take steps to make his listening habits and ability the best he can make them.

Question . . . Then Listen!

Modern successful selling techniques involve the skillful questioning of prospects to bring out their needs and desires, to find the real objections, to lead them into making their own decisions favorable to the sale. The preceding chapter, "Selling Through Questioning," gives suggestions for developing this skill. But the job is only half done by skillful questioning. The salesman must LISTEN just as skillfully to detect the true meaning of the reply and to keep from missing important information that can lead to the sale and satisfaction for the customer.

Bill Watson called on the same prospect that several other photo copier salesmen had called on. He heard the same reason for not buying: business was off. But by really listening, he also heard that "things might be different if we can get a good contract." Six weeks later, Bill read that the firm had won a bid on a new building. He called the prospect, reminded him of the previous interview, made an appointment for a demonstration, and closed the sale for three new copiers. The key fact was buried under the same old talk, but Bill alone was *listening.*

Many universities, colleges and high schools are offering courses in listening to help students get more out of their class lectures and discussions. In some schools this is a required course during the indoctrination period or first year. Dr. Ralph Nichols, an authority on communications and a pioneer in listening studies at the University of Minnesota declares, "There are no uninteresting subjects, just *uninterested listeners.*"

Why Doesn't a Salesman Really Listen?

A salesman has the same problems with listening as any other person. But since his career depends upon getting the right information from his prospects and customers, it is more important that he recognizes these problems and does something about them.

Based on research in communications, we can boil down the salesman's problems in listening into three primary categories:

1. **He doesn't pay attention.** Being a good listener takes work, so we avoid it if we can. It always presents questions that need answering, problems that need solving. We feel we could use the time to better advantage, like preparing what we're going to say when the talker gets through.

Have you ever been guilty of faking attention to the speaker while your mind wandered all over the lot? This happens particularly when the subject matter isn't entertaining. We resist the toil of brainwork.

Distractions take their toll on the listening quality of the salesman, too. Some of this can't be avoided, like the entrance of a captivating secretary. But some can be tuned out with a little effort.

2. **He misses the real point.** Sometimes the salesman becomes more interested in a prospect's mannerisms, clothes, accent, or voice and misses what he is really saying.

A listener can also pay so much attention to getting bits of facts that he misses the real meaning. Facts out of context can cause a misunderstanding or result in a wrong conclusion.

3. **He permits his emotions to interfere.** Emotion is a barrier to comprehension. It can make us hostile to the speaker's point of view, or it can make us unduly enthusiastic about it. Emotions are difficult to control, but when the salesman knows what they will do, he can recognize his reactions and say to himself, "Wait a minute, better calm down and look at the facts for what they are."

11 Ways to Improve Your Listening Skills

Many firms now have courses in listening skill for their salesmen, managers and other employees. Anyone whose success depends upon working with or through others can do a better job after observing and practicing some simple rules and techniques. These courses usually cover several hours of discussion and practice and may extend over a period of several weeks.

We will give the basic principles for more effective listening here, but the key to success is *putting them into practice* through conscientious determination at every opportunity to listen.

1. **Take time to listen.** The inexperienced salesman sometimes feels that he's not selling when he isn't talking, so he gets into the habit of taking over the interview with his own talk, forcing the prospect to listen. Some talking is necessary, of course, but seldom more than 50% of the interview. Much can be learned by getting the prospect to talk. Some good salesmen make it a rule to avoid talking more than a minute at a time unless they have given the buyer a chance to say something.

If the buyer cuts in, stop talking and listen. If you don't, the buyer probably won't hear another word you say anyway. Nothing is as interesting as what he's waiting to say.

If the prospect asks a question, don't be too quick with the answer. Wait a few seconds to at least show that you are considering the question a fair one and want to give a good answer. And you might just give a better answer if you force yourself to wait three seconds. If you wait, you are also more sure that the prospect has finished talking.

2. **Pay Attention.** A light doesn't go on until you flip the switch. Before you can listen to a person, you have to flip your attention switch. Be open-eared and open-minded. Everyone finds that giving full attention to most things is difficult, there are so many other things that can crowd the immediate action out of our conscious mind. But to be a good listener, the salesman has to push his worries and plans into the background to make room for what his prospect is saying. When you find your mind wandering — and it will if you're normal — pull it back sharply, telling yourself, "Look, fellow, if you're going to learn anything from what this guy is saying, you'd better pay attention!"

The customer wants attention, he wants to be listened to. All the more reason to give him your *full* attention. Acknowledge what he says by giving some reply by word, gesture of facial expression. Don't mystify or antagonize him with a blank expression, doodling or playing with articles around you.

3. **Fight off distractions.** The degree to which distractions keep us from listening depends upon our interest in the subject. Unless the salesman is aware of the pull of distractions, he can become more involved in criticizing the prospect's clothes, his delivery, his voice, his beard, the smell of his pipe, than in listening to what he is saying.

4. **Watch those emotions.** Keep your mind open, don't let it close up because of emotional words or actions used by the prospect or customer. A former customer quits buying from you and you try to get him back in the fold. He quit, he says, "because you stupid jerks tried to unload a bunch of junk on me." Now your emotions tell you to fight back in kind, but if you remember that emotions keep you from listening for clues to make the sale, you'll fight the urge and ask questions that lead him to get the venom out of his system and to thinking about some reasons for buying from your firm again. As a starter, you might say, "You must have really been upset. Would you tell me what happened?" As he talks, he lets off steam and gives clues to show that all is not lost. Listen for them, clues like: "Your stuff is usually good, but . . ." or: "Even if it does cost less, I made up my mind that . . ." But you won't be able to hear these clues if you let your own emotions take control.

Excitement can give the salesman almost as much trouble in listening. The expectation of making a sale frequently makes the salesman appear overanxious, nervous or impatient. This makes the buyer cautious. The salesman must force the appearance of relaxation while retaining enthusiasm. A good way is to really listen and express interest in what the prospect is saying.

5. **Persuade while listening.** When we listen to a speaker on a platform, we have to listen to his entire presentation without personal involvement. He doesn't need us. But the salesman listens to very short speeches, perhaps only a few seconds in length. So part of his listening job is to get the prospect into talking some more, to draw him out, to get more information he can listen to.

The salesman persuades in two important ways, by giving his obvious attention to what the prospect says, and by asking questions that probe deeper into the problem or desire. The section on "Selling Through Questioning" (page 55) deals with such questions.

6. **Put yourself in the prospect's shoes.** The successful salesman likes people. When you like people, you like to listen to them, their desires and their problems. By asking questions and listening, the salesman develops empathy with his prospect, defined by the dictionary as "mentally entering into the feeling and spirit of a person." When you put yourself into the prospect's shoes, another way of describing empathy, you put yourself in a better position to help him solve his problem.

Studies have shown that the primary reason why people stop buying from a firm is because the sales people are indifferent to their desires. Listening will help keep the good customers as well as attract the new ones. Henry Ford said, "If there is any one secret of success, it lies in the ability to get the other person's point of view and see things from his angle as well as from your own."

7. **Listen for keys to the sale.** The key to maintaining interest in what the prospect is saying is to ask yourself, "What's he saying that I can use to make the sale?" Of course, we're thinking of "sale" here in its best sense, the satisfaction of the customer's needs and wants. So the salesman listens for key expressions of needs, wants and desires in what the prospect is saying.

8. **Focus on ideas, not facts alone.** When a salesman determines to listen to his prospect, he may make the mistake of trying to remember a list of facts. Certain facts, of course, are important, like size, quantities, colors, etc. But the salesman must not concentrate so much on retaining facts that he overlooks the underlying purpose or desire the prospect has that can be satisfied by the right product. The salesman for

office equipment notes that the prospect is interested in a desk and chair, but he also gets the underlying idea that the prospect likes prestige styling more than he does low cost. The salesman may have to probe a bit with questions to get the big idea, but he can do this when he realizes that he must not be content to listen for facts alone.

9. **Listen between the words.** When you studied the section "Why People Buy" (page 6), you were reminded that people don't always say what they really mean about buying or not buying a product. When listening to a prospect, therefore, the salesman doesn't take a statement like "I can't afford it," at face value. He listens for clues as to why the prospect is really hesitating, where he needs to do some reselling, what new appeal he needs to project.

10. **Take notes.** You can't, nor should you try to, take notes on every conversation with a prospect. But where correct facts and data are important, don't trust to memory.

11. **Feed back.** A group of people can listen to the same thing and come up with a variety of meanings or facts. While this phenomenon makes a good party game, it should also make the salesman wary of what he thinks he's hearing. The best technique from several angles is to repeat back to the prospect the gist of what he said. "Now let me see if I understand your problem, Mr. Gross." The salesman may find that he really didn't understand. If he did, this technique encourages the prospect to reassess what he said, to listen to the salesman, and to feel that the salesman is really interested.

Selling Is Persuasive Communication

Skillful listening is at least half of the requirement for successful communication. All the salesman's artful presentation, his penetrating questioning to probe hidden needs and desires of the prospect, lose their great potential for selling success when the salesman neglects to match them with equal skill in listening to his prospect.

The techniques and suggestions for more profitable listening which we have discussed here have put salesmen into high levels of professional accomplishment. But they will be only interesting reading unless you put them into practice, and practice, and practice. It is not easy to listen when you want to talk. But it is worth the effort if you want a successful career in selling.

Handling Problem Customers

YOUR selling job would be a bed of roses if it weren't for people! Only trouble of course is that without people, you won't make any sales, earn any money, or eat. So the only practical solution for the salesman is to get along with people and so make more money, eat better and end up getting more fun out of selling.

Getting along with all types of prospects and customers requires an important quality in a salesman — tact. You'll find tact high on most lists of qualities the good salesman should have. Webster defines tact as a "keen sense of what to say or do to avoid giving offense." We might call it the lubrication in the selling machine.

An important part of your selling approach — even the pre-approach — is the classification of your prospect. A "canned" approach will not work the same way on the various prospect and customer types. Classification of your customers will come in handy when they start to raise objections. Once you have determined a customer's or prospect's temperament and mental habits, you will be able to handle his objections in the right manner. As we discuss the various customer types, you will see that to handle them all alike could amount to sales suicide.

12 Problem Customers and How to Handle Them

It takes all kinds of customers to make a selling world. As you go through your selling day you will meet as many different kinds of customers as there are human minds. It would be impossible and impractical to classify them all precisely, but we can break them down into 12 common groups for speedy recognition and satisfactory handling when we encounter them.

The Arguer. He's ready to argue at the drop of your hat. He likes to get you involved, so keep away from side issues and personalities. Stick to your proposition. Above all, don't try to win an argument and lose the sale. Keep cool and calm. Listen courteously and use his own arguments to prove your point. "You're perfectly right, Mr. Wallace, safety is very important. That's why this framis is made of tough nylon that won't wear out and allow the assembly to bind."

The Put-It-Off. He doesn't believe in ordering today what he can put off until your next trip. He's the one customer you're justified in applying a little "high pressure" to. For his own good, of course. Point out how much he will save by buying now, what will happen if he runs out of stock, how much labor costs he will save each day that he owns your item and how this is lost each day he is without it.

The Price Buyer. He really cries when he can't buy it wholesale. Play with him by his rules and you lose your shirt! Your best protection against the price buyer is to know your full costs. Don't give your profits away; there's no advantage in trading dollars. Sell him on the additional quality and service which justifies the price. If this doesn't work, you are better off to set a firm, take-it-or-leave figure and use your time on more profitable customers.

The Penny-Pincher. Don't confuse this guy with the Price Buyer. He will pay the full dollar if he is certain that he gets a full dollar's value.

Compliment his ability to recognize value, then prove the value of your goods. Appeal to his pride. Don't question his judgment.

The Clam. He's the toughest customer of all. If silence were golden, he'd be another Fort Knox. He makes you think you're talking to yourself — but he really does listen. The Clam really loosens *your* tongue if you're not careful, and your yakety-yak can talk you right out of a sale. Best attack is to stick to your regular sales presentation. Ask him leading questions, ones that call for a definite expression of an opinion — a yes opinion of course. The Clam is usually a thinker, and a short, sensible sales presentation will impress him more than a flood of words. Don't hesitate in trying to close the sale just because he doesn't talk. Just one word — yes — is all you need to get out of him.

The Shopper. "I'll look around and let you know." When you let the Shopper go with this statement, the chances are very good you'll never hear from him again. Some other salesman is going to show him that he is wasting important time and money by unnecessary shopping. He's going to have so much proof and argument piled upon him that he will be overwhelmed and buy without coming back to you. Why take chances? You might as well be the salesman that stops him in his tracks. Many salesmen succeed with him by simply asking, "What can you gain by shopping except lost time, worn nerves and tired feet? You agree that the price is right, you like the color, and it definitely fits your need. And when you buy it from a reputable firm like ours, you can bring it back if it isn't right." If he still insists on shopping, be sure to review your selling features and benefits with him to increase the chances of his coming back.

The Smarty-Pants. You can't tell him anything! He knows it all and he wants you to realize it. He likes to hear himself talk, so let him sell himself. When he mentions a feature, agree with him. "You really seem to know this product. That's one of our best features. I wish all my customers were as quick to see its advantages as you are." When he runs down, simply ask for the order.

The Deliberate Customer. He's got lots of patience and likes to consider every angle. He might be slow, but he's not necessarily dull-witted. He merely thinks more thoroughly. Actually, he is a good customer to have because he will listen to your proposition, consider it thoroughly, and give you a square deal. Don't confuse him with the Put-It-Off. He may exasperate you with his procrastination, but if you have done a better job of establishing the value of your product than the other salesmen, you will get the sale. That's more than you can hope for with the impulsive customer. Slow up your presentation. Don't rush the deliberate customer or he becomes stubborn. You have to know your merchandise thoroughly and present selling features in detail. Above all, you have to have patience.

The Impulsive Customer. He is the typical "ants-in-the-pants" fellow. He has a lot of things to do and has a hard time concentrating on what you are saying. He shuffles his papers, drums his pencil, looks at his watch. He can tell you he's not interested before you get started on your presentation. This impulsive customer can be rushed, in contrast to the deliberate customer above. Give a fast sales talk, hitting the high spots, then ask for the order. If he turns you down, no harm done. Go into a more detailed presentation of the points in which he showed an interest. He's a man of action and he likes salesmen who are men of action. Don't make the mistake of boring him. Here's a particularly good spot for case histories — "Let me show you what Acme is doing in its shipping department." Anything that grabs his interest or gets him into the act will keep him with you.

The Tough Guy. He's usually the self-made businessman, positive, confident, decided. He's often egotistical and overbearing. This type thinks he knows it all, and the best selling tactic is to let him continue to think so. Don't show him up, prove him wrong, or hurt his pride. Ask his opinion, get him to do the talking. Above all, don't try to *sell* him. He prefers to *give* the order. Find something to praise him for, the size of his operation, the beauty of his buildings, the smooth operation. Be sure the praise is legitimate, because he will rebel at any obvious soft-soaping. Nice thing about the "tough guy": if you get him for a customer, the next salesman will have a hard time getting him away from you.

The Friendly Customer. Bless him! He'll talk and smile about anything. He's like an oasis on a hot desert. Trouble is you may waste a lot of time gossiping with him only to find he has smiled you right out of his office without the order. But he's fine to do business with. Just match his smile and his optimism. Be forthright in your presentation, play to his sense of fairness. Just don't be lulled into leaving his office without trying to close an order.

Old Faithful. You don't have near enough of this type of customer. He depends on you for all his needs. He doesn't listen to competitive salesmen because you have convinced him that your quality-service-price combination can't be beat. The hitch is that you can't pick him out of your list at first. He might be any one of the other 11 types we have just talked about. But when you identified him properly and handled him right, he became Old Faithful. But watch out! Like the wild animals at the zoo, he can revert to type in an instant if you take him for granted and forget to use the right selling method.

Keeping
Your
Customers

H OW much is an old customer worth? Look over your sales record for last month and see what percentage of your sales came from regular customers. If you are a typical salesman who has been selling a reasonable length of time, you may find that as much as 75 percent of your sales and commissions came from these people.

Are they worth keeping?

If you ask a businessman what his company is worth, he will multiply his annual sales volume by ten to get an approximation of his firm's capital value. Use the same rule of thumb on your customers. How many customers do you have who buy regularly? What is their total annual volume? Multiply by ten and you have a capital asset, your loyal customers. Is this worth protecting?

What are you doing to keep your faithful customers?

Stop Trading Customers!

Here is a salesman who seems to spend most of his time trading customers with his competitors? This week he is working hard to win the Jones Co. away from a rival. He finally succeeds, but meanwhile he neglected the Brown Co. — and another competitor took it away from him. Trading dollars is not much of an investment. Neither is trading customers!

Yes, there is a "thrill of the chase" atmosphere about finding new prospects. When the prospect is converted to a customer, some salesmen feel as if the fun is gone. They neglect the domesticated customer for the wild game prospect still at large. This kind of selling is fine if selling is merely a sport with you. But if you are interested in higher commissions and profits, you need to turn your attention to the domesticated customer.

Before we go too far, let's make sure that we understand that new accounts are important, too. You have to gain new accounts not only to grow but to stand still, hold your ground. Even the best salesmen lose 10 to 15 per cent of their customers each year through no fault of their own. The development of new accounts is an important part of your selling activity — and survival. What we are focusing on here, however, is the importance of your present customer, how to keep him, and how to make him more profitable.

Because of that wonderful sales stimulant called "confidence," it's much easier to sell to a regular customer than to a new one. In the case of a new customer, time and experience are necessary before confidence can enter the relationship.

With proper cultivation, it is possible for a business firm to make more profit on a smaller volume with *established* customers than on a larger volume of *new* business. Here are some reasons why this is so.

1. A salesman is tempted to sell the cheaper lines to land a new account. He sells the better lines to established accounts at a higher profit.

2. Orders from new accounts are usually too small to be profitable.

3. Credit losses are higher on new customers.

4. Returns and adjustments are lower with old customers because

of their better understanding of the merchandise and company policies.

5. On new accounts expense is out of proportion to sales.

The Salesman Takes a "Wife"

The salesman-customer relations is quite similar to that of husband and wife in many respects. You have the courtship, during which you put on your very best behavior. You employ your very best selling techniques. Then you make the sale — you "marry" the customer. During the honeymoon, you shower your new customer-bride with attention, and everything is bliss.

But, like some husbands, you may start neglecting your bride after the honeymoon. You spend too much time away from the customer when you should be building up more business. Just about the time the customer-bride feels a little neglected, the villain competitor slinks out of the shadows, becomes very attentive, and wins the young bride away.

If you are the wise salesman-husband, however, you will continue to show the respect and attention which the true customer deserves. While you do that, no competitor looks nearly so attractive! Keep using the same salesmanship you used to land the customer. Treat each call as a new sale. Be enthusiastic. Bring samples, offer something new, try to expand the purchases, offer more services. You know some of the customer's requirements. Cater to them. Find out what his other requirements are and try to fill them.

A 5-Step Customer-Conservation Program

There's nothing complicated about keeping customers. No customer will leave you as long as it is to his advantage to stay. Your job is to make sure that there is an advantage in the continued relationship, and that your customer is aware of it.

The only reason some salesmen lose good customers is the lack of any systematic determination to keep them. Once they decide to do something about it, these salesmen find that all they need to do is give the customer the attention he deserves. Here are the steps to take in setting up a realistic customer conservation program:

1. **Identify your customers.** Who are they? Anyone who buys from you, no matter how occasionally.

2. **How much are they buying?** Write down the annual volume you get from each customer on your list.

3. **Rate each customer.** Rate your customers A-B-C-D according to their purchase volume as described on page 80, in "Planning Your Selling Time." Time your customer calls and devote your attention according to each customer's potential. Spend more time, call more often on the A customers. If you have to slight any, slight the D customers.

4. **Analyze.** Your ABCD ratings show the relative value of each customer to you now. Ask yourself some questions about each one. How can I raise this B customer to an A customer, or a C to B. How much of this customer's total business am I getting? Am I spending enough time on this valuable customer to keep him? Should this customer be buying more lines from me?

5. **Plan your action.** Set up a definite program aimed at: (a) making small customers bigger, (b) getting all the possible business from a regular customer, (c) making a now-and-then buyer a regular customer.

6 Ways to Keep Your Customers

If you consolidated all the things a good salesman should do to keep his valuable customers on his side, you would find that they pretty well fall into these six rules:

1. **Know your customer well.** Many salesmen keep a customer diary in which they enter comments about the customer — about his special needs, likes, dislikes, hobbies, family, special interests. With a record like this, you would have a better chance of pleasing your customers. Pleased customers continue to give orders.

2. **Contact him often.** Make as many calls as you can, as often as you can. You need to regulate this technique of course, by considerations regarding the time spent with the customer and the relative worth of his account and those of other customers. Personal calls are best, naturally, but make use of telephone calls, letters, and notes to keep the customer aware of your desire to serve him properly. Some salesmen even send personal cards to customers while away on vacation.

3. **Handle complaints promptly.** No salesman cultivates complaints, but they are a wonderful opportunity to cement customer relations. Don't take any complaint lightly, no matter how trivial it may seem to you or how chronic the complaint may be. This doesn't mean giving in to every demand a customer makes — only that you should make it obvious to the customer that you will conscientiously do what you can to settle his complaint.

Don't pass the buck on complaints. Back up your firm's policies and prices, but do make every effort to see that your customer gets proper treatment. If someone else in your firm erred, take the bitter medicine as part of your responsibility as a salesman. Passing the buck lowers the customer's estimation of both you and the firm. After you are sure that the customer is satisfied with your handling of his complaint, ask for another order. This is very important, for it establishes the fact that you and the customer are still happy with your association.

4. **Prove that you are dependable.** Make promises—then keep them. You can't prove that you're dependable unless you make promises, despite all you might have been told about the danger of making promises and the security in not making them. Little promises kept may not be important in themselves to the customer, but your dependability for keeping your promise is!

5. **Serve him "to death!"** This is a selling key emphasized by Bill Gove, winner of the Salesman-of-the-Year Award from the National Sales Executive Club. No customer will leave you as long as he can't afford to! Make yourself indispensable by looking for things to do for your customer. Give him any kind of assistance you can.

6. **Show your appreciation.** We all like to feel important, and your customer is no exception. Parents will do more for a child who shows his appreciation — it inflates the ego, makes them feel good. Similarly, do favors for your customers in appreciation. Even *ask* for small favors. We are all flattered when someone asks us a favor, and our reward is their show of appreciation.

So You Lost a Customer

So far in this story, we have talked about preventing the loss of a customer. We hope that it works 100 per cent, but we suspect that it won't. You're going to lose a good customer now and then. What are you going to do about it?

You could be nonchalant, shrug it off, do nothing. After all, he was the one who quit. Let him suffer. You can get more customers. Why should you go crawling back?

Funny thing. You don't hear successful salesmen talking like that. They immediately take action, accepting the lost customer as a challenge to their selling skill. Take a tip from them. Follow these steps to win the customer back into the fold.

1. *Contact him first.* Get to the customer before your competitors do.

Like a disillusioned lover, he might do something foolish, then be too stubborn to go back.

2. *Find out what happened.* Be sure you get the real reason. Then offer to make amends.

3. *Invite him to come back.* Earnestly tell him that you don't want to lose him, that you value his business, that you still like him. Like the rest of us, customers sometimes make quick decisions they wish they could take back. But pride stands in the way. Make it easy for him to save face, to do you a favor, and be your customer again.

4. *Keep calling.* If you don't win him back immediately, ask permission to keep calling anyway. There's a big temptation for any salesman to quit a customer cold after losing him. After all, we have our pride, too. But if the customer was worth having in the first place, he is worth trying to have again. Treat the customer as a prospect. This kind of sportsmanship does much to gain the customer's respect and to regain the lost account. Don't give up. Keep calling. Keep pleasant. Keep trying to be helpful. Keep selling. Time heals even the deepest wounds!

Planning Your Selling Time

A SUCCESSFUL salesman, like the owner or manager of a company, depends upon good management. How he plans his work, uses his time, organizes his knowledge and skills can be more important than any unusual skill in selling fundamentals alone.

In many ways, the salesman is in business for himself. If he is a good manager of himself and his assets, he will prosper. If he cannot or will not manage himself, he will stay small or fail. The salesman is not under direct supervision like the typical man at a desk. He must do much of his own supervision, disciplining himself to spend his time profitably, plan his work, set objectives, keep records, analyze his performance and make the necessary adjustments and improvements that lead to success.

Hard work alone is not enough for success, although it is one of the necessary ingredients. The salesman's efforts must be controlled and directed for maximum efficiency in the use of time and the development of his territory.

TIME — the Salesman's Investment

Time is the salesman's investment in his "business." How he uses it determines the rate of return on his investment. He can't afford to waste it. He must use it where it will bring the largest net return in profitable sales.

You must plan your investment of time just as a financier plans his investment of money. You must place every portion of time available in your selling day into the use which brings you the greatest return in commissions.

If you are a typical salesman, you spend only 15 per cent of your day in front of your customers. You spend 40 per cent of your time getting to the customers, 20 per cent waiting for them, and 25 per cent on personal matters and detail work.

If you can whittle only 18 minutes a day from the non-productive travel, waiting, and personal work, you automatically increase your selling time over 25 per cent!

You have heard the selling axiom: to make more sales, you have to make more calls. We can't argue much with this principle because the law of averages hasn't been repealed yet. Nor can we argue with this corollary of the axiom: you will make more profit and more commissions if you plan your calls so that they give you a better return on your time investment. What's more, fewer but more selective calls will produce a more profitable return on your investment than many haphazard calls.

There is a definite place in your sales plan for the "cold canvass" and a part of your selling time should be set aside for systematic screening of your territory to uncover those prospects who seem to elude all other forms of selection. But the salesman who knows the value of planned selling, picks his primary prospects according to the potential business he has a reasonable chance of securing. If a prospect would still be unprofitable even if you were to get all his business, you can't afford to waste much time on him.

There is a hitch to every program in selling, and you have already thought of the one that fits into this picture. How do you *know* which prospects are good for profitable sales? The answer must be that you don't . . . for sure. But your educated "guesstimates" will prove most reliable. Save the borderline cases and the questionable ones for the times when you want to cold-canvass, when you have made a comfortable quota and you are now ready to beat the bushes for the ones that you temporarily allowed to get away.

Make a Call Frequency Schedule

Salesmen with experience in a particular territory can budget the amount of time they spend on each regular customer call. For a guide, they set an average sale figure as a minimum requirement for each call. Then they rate each customer on their call list according to his sales potential for the year. By asking the question, "How often do I need to call on this customer to average a reasonable sale?", the salesman sets up several customer classifications.

Bill Drake, an office supplies and equipment salesman, might decide that he has to average $50 in sales per call to maintain the income he wants. How often should he call on his regular customers to maintain this average without slighting any or taking too much time on others?

Bill might decide to break his regular customers into four classifications, A-B-C-D, according to their annual potential, and set up a call schedule something like this:

CLASS	ANNUAL SALES POTENTIAL	CALL SCHEDULE
A	Over $2,000	Every two weeks or oftener
B	$1,000 to $2,000	Monthly
C	$500 to $1,000	Every six weeks
D	Under $500	Two to four times a year

Bill might have made more than four classifications and provided for once-a-week and once-every-three-week calls, but this is probably sufficient to help in his planning. He can easily determine the customers he needs to call on more than once every two weeks, for example. And there may be some customers in Class D with promising potential whom he may want to call on once a month, just to keep in better touch. He will use telephone calls and direct mail advertising to supplement the less frequent personal calls.

Each salesman needs to plan his own customer classifications and call frequency schedules because of such varying factors as type of product or service, unit sale, salesman's compensation plan, time required to make the sale, territory coverage, etc. Some salesmen may have to average a much larger sale per call than our example, some may make out with less. A $2,500-a-year customer for some salesmen might be in their Class D schedule.

The important thing is that a call schedule based upon sales potential keeps the salesman from wasting time on the less profitable accounts and helps him put his time where it counts the most.

Concentrate on your profitable customers to get all their business. What if your competitors steal the little ones away in the meantime? Since the amount of time available may make some loss inevitable, better the small ones than the large ones.

Planning the Calls

After the customer list is thoroughly established on the basis of sales potential, set up a schedule. You will end up with several schedules — yearly, monthly, weekly, and daily.

You won't have a complete yearly schedule, of course, but you will have some broad plan that will bring all your customers and prospects under coverage throughout the year. If a customer's sales potential is such that he merits a call every two months, or maybe four times a year, you need some schedule that reminds you to call on him within that time.

The monthly and weekly schedules are more definite and permit changes in plans caused by selling conditions. The weekly schedule is completed by Saturday of the preceding week as a rule, having been built all during that week by such notes as, "See Jones of Acme next Wednesday at 10."

Many salesmen like to keep Friday for clean-up or prospecting. A part of each day may also be devoted to prospecting, as time permits. If you plan to be in a particular area on Tuesday, allow yourself a little time to make a few prospect calls while in the area. This saves time and travel later, and is insurance that you will make the call.

Your daily schedule tells you each morning where you are going during the day and the shortest route that will get you there. Calls are arranged to minimize backtracking.

6 Records for the Salesman

Records are essential for the salesman if he is to plan and control his activity efficiently. The time required to keep them is justified by the improvement that takes place in the quality of the salesman's selling. A record is worth keeping only if it is designed and maintained so that its information can be used effectively. Useless details should be eliminated. Daily reports should be made out after each call to give fresh facts, avoid errors.

While the salesman will naturally keep whatever records his company requires, he will also keep whatever records of his own that will contribute to his success. Here are six typical salesman records.

1. **Prospects and Customers.** These are kept separately, but they are similar in form and maintenance. They contain a history of the salesman's attention to and experience with each actual and prospective account.

2. **Daily Calls.** This tells the salesman whom he has called on, and the results. It gives facts that help on the next call, some of which can be transferred to the prospect and customer records. While the information is usually kept on record cards, some salesmen keep customer records in individual folders.

3. **Sales Record.** Record should break down total sales to give information for better sales concentration. Then be classified by product line or price line. Or by day, week and month. Or size of order, type of buyer, type of sale. Whatever the breakdown, it must give the salesman information that will help him plan his selling time to get a higher volume of profitable sales.

4. **Expenses.** The firm that refunds expenses and the Internal Revenue Bureau which allows tax credit, require an expense record. The breakdown must be detailed enough to permit analysis and comparison, but broad enough to be reasonable in preparation and recording time.

5. **Time.** While the daily call record will give an idea of how the salesman spends his time, a time record tells exactly how much time the salesman is spending on each of his activities. The long-range benefit is that he cuts out non-essentials, manages his remaining time to spend more of it in the presence of buyers. The time record is seldom a permanent fixture but rather one for newer salesmen, a new territory, or for occasional checking by the experienced salesman.

6. **Tickler File.** A tickler file with folders numbered for each day in the month, tells the salesman whom to see and things to do each day. Some of the data he needs can be placed in the tickler folder, but much of the information will be in the prospect and customer files. After the

daily calls, the salesman drops data on his future calls into the appropriate tickler folders.

4 Ways to Increase Sales Volume

If you are not satisfied with your present sales volume, there are only four ways in which you can improve it.

1. Work longer hours.
2. Increase face-to-face selling time.
3. Invest your time where it counts most.
4. Increase the effectiveness of your selling performance.

If you study these four solutions, you see that time is the one factor that runs through all of them. Basic to improving your sales volume, then, is better utilization of your time.

Working longer hours is perhaps the weakest solution of the four. You cannot get more than twenty-four hours a day, and you can't stretch them. And there is a point where long hours break down your efficiency and your health. So a better solution is to do a better job with the hours you do have available — better time management.

The suggestions and ideas which follow are related to increasing your *time before customers* and putting your time investment where it counts the most. Spending time to improve your skill and knowledge and reviewing your performance is obviously a key factor in improving your success as a salesman. You will find many aids for this important job throughout this book.

47 HINTS FOR BETTER TIME MANAGEMENT

Here is a valuable collection of suggestions for saving time and making better use of the time available. They have been used by successful salesmen from all over the country.

Don't expect to put all the ideas to work at once. Read them all, select the ones that are easiest to put to work immediately. Then review the list from time to time to get gradual improvement in your selling efficiency.

Plan Your Time

1. Know exactly where you are going and why — before you leave the office each morning.

2. Do your planning and paper work before and after the best selling hours of the day, and on weekends. Save the best hours of each day for actual selling.

3. Schedule your time, monthly, weekly, daily.

4. Determine the best time to interview certain buyers. Schedule calls and appointments for these times and build the other calls around them.

5. Make evening appointments when the husband is home if your product or service is a consumer item.

6. Don't depend upon theories that sales can't be made on certain days or times. Other salesmen make them before 10, after a holiday, on Saturdays, on bad weather days, after closing, during the lunch hour. Some customers may have definite off-times. No general rules apply.

7. Fill in schedule with cold calls and prospecting in the same areas as customer calls. Do not let them get in the way of more profitable customer calls, however.

8. Keep office routine to a minimum. Don't let it unnecessarily keep you from making the first call in the morning.

9. Screen prospects. Call on those first that are most likely to buy.

10. Base frequency of calls on potential rather than convenience. Give more attention, calls, time to the more profitable accounts.

11. Budget your time for one important project, but stop when the time goes too far beyond the budget to be practical. If you don't, you rob valuable time from your next project or task.

12. Keep in contact with the office regularly to get word of changes or developments that might affect your schedule, save a wasted trip, produce something you might want to show a customer.

13. Firm up your next day's schedule the evening before.

14. Follow up with phone calls as you go along to confirm arrangements and to make new appointments.

15. When waiting is inevitable, catch up on your planning and record-keeping.

16. Be flexible enough to absorb changes and cancellations. Have fill-ins ready for substitutions, second choices for back-up.

17. Study each day's performance. Where could it be improved? Take steps to improve your efficiency.

Travel Time

1. Reduce your travel time by routing your daily calls so as to avoid backtracking.

2. Plan each day's work to concentrate your effort in areas that take a minimum amount of travel time.

3. Select the method of transportation best suited for the area to be covered — private car, taxi, walking in some instances.

4. Use a map to lay out the day's calls, and mark it.

5. Plan for travel and meals, wherever possible, while the buyers are having lunch.

Personal Time

1. Watch the coffee breaks, the long meal times, the slow starts in the morning, the early quits in the afternoon. The time before the customer is what counts most.

2. Avoid the impulse to goof off after a good sale or after a string of unprofitable ones.

3. Don't succumb to "bad weather blues". Keep making calls.

4. Don't put it off. The job or project that is put off for no good reason seldom gets done at all.

5. Don't manufacture excuses. You can always find reasons for not doing something, or for not doing it now. Set a time to do the job, and do it when that time comes.

6. Learn to say No! Don't take on odd jobs with the firm that will reduce your available amount of face-to-face selling time without weighing the advantages of your total selling success.

7. Don't become a delivery boy. Customer service is essential to a point, but don't get into the habit of using valuable selling time for non-essential customer work that could be turned over to someone else in the firm.

8. Be a good citizen and participate in community affairs. But be willing to say no when the requests for time-consuming committee work get to the point of interfering with your selling and planning time. Budget the time you spend on outside activities, your home and family, and your job. Give each one a fair share.

Before the Call

1. Make appointments by telephone or letter to insure the interviews and avoid waiting time and wasted effort.

2. Make appointments *at least* for the first and last calls of the day to make sure that you start and end on a planned schedule.

3. Send advance letters and literature to prepare the prospect. This reduces the presentation time.

4. Eliminate wasted calls by critical analysis of the need for certain calls.

5. Use the telephone for customer calls that need not be made in person.

6. Before walking into the customer's office, check the customer record to review data on previous calls, needs, etc. This will eliminate small talk while you are getting organized.

7. Have all presentation material in order and complete to prevent fumbling and waste motion during the call.

During the Call

1. Prepare the sales presentation carefully to minimize the time necessary to close the sale.

2. Get right to the purpose of the call during the interview. Personal chatter has occasional merit, but don't let it eat up productive selling time.

3. Close as many sales as possible in the first interview.

4. Listen and take notes. Listen to the prospect's reactions, take notes of the details to insure that you won't have to make an extra call later on to fill a gap in your information.

Keep Records

1. Maintain and study records at times other than the selling day — early morning, evening, weekends.

2. Fill out call report after each call to be sure you have all the facts, time for next call, etc. This can save needless calls or wasted calls later.

3. Keep a sales record to see where your sales volume is coming from — which accounts, which merchandise. Compare results with time spent on each account. Are some not worth the time? Can some be developed if you had more time?

4. Keep a time record at least for a reasonable period to see where your daily time goes. Study the patterns to see what can be eliminated, shortened. Account for each minute, charging it to planning, personal, travel, waiting, selling, record keeping, etc.

5. Keep a tickler file with folders 1 to 31 for each day in the month. This will keep you from forgetting appointments, important details, will save time in planning.

6. Keep customer and prospect record cards to minimize planning time, and to place your concentration where it counts most.

Work Your Plan

It's not easy to plan your selling time and carry your plan through.

We all like to dawdle over one more cigarette, to stop in for a cup of coffee, to call it a day after a few good sales, to talk too long about our golf game to an interested customer. But every minute that ticks off between 8 and 5:30 either adds to or takes away from the return on your investment.

Planning your work is important if you want to make more sales and more commissions. But you must work your plans as well as you plan your work! Regiment yourself to follow through.

Analyze your plan when you have finished part of it. Make changes. Regroup your resources and resourcefulness for the next attack. Don't be discouraged when you lose a battle. It's the final victory that's important and to the victor goes the big commissions.

Are you using these *other books* by Homer Smith?

Selling Through Negotiation

The salesperson's handbook for *Sales Negotiation*. How to combine negotiating and selling skills to close more sales. How to cope with 24 tactics buyers are trained to use to get lower prices and more concessions from you. 18 strategies for handling concessions. 6 trade-offs to ask for in exchange for a concession. 19 techniques for handling buyer resistance. Full chapter on *how* to *use questions in every step of the sale* with lots of examples. Much more. Hard cover, $19.95; paperback $14.95. Volume discounts.

How to Critique Your Own Sales Calls

Homer Smith and Jared Harrison were among the pioneers of what was called the *Curbside Conference* technique sales managers could use to constructively critique their salespeople's performance immediately after a call and motivate them to improve. But managers don't have time to go out with their salespeople as much as they should, so Smith and Harrison converted their successful technique to a method salespeople can use to *critique their own sales calls*. Basic is a Checksheet covering all six stages of the typical sales call. The authors lead the salesperson through EVERY question on the Checklist, giving reasons for asking the question, then suggesting ways to pinpoint problems and arrive at specific solutions to use the next time. The Checklist and a Sales Call Planning Worksheet are bound in the center of the book for easy removal for reproducing as many copies as desired. $6.95

Organizing for Better Meetings

The all-time best-seller handbook for planning sales meetings; seminars; distributor meetings; new product demonstrations; convention programs; and management meetings. Published by *Sales & Marketing Management* magazine, now available only from MEA.. Guidelines and 450-point checklists for every meeting requirement prevent embarrassing and costly slipups. Covers basic steps in planning any meeting like negotiating meeting sites; meeting room layouts; audio-visual aids; handling speakers; budgeting and ways to cut costs. Provides specific ideas for programs including *167 sales meeting topics. 88 stunts to liven up meetings. Group participation techniques; How to conduct special types of meeting segments like conferences; seminars; cases; role-play; skits; panels; buzz sessions; in-basket exercises; brainstorming; and others. 105-page, 8 1/2 x 11-inch, spiral--bound handbook.* $9.95

Marketing Education Associates
4004 Rosemary Street – Chevy Chase, MD 20815
(301) 656-5550 E-mail: homsmith@erols.com

TO The WaBon FamiLY
Thanks For Your
SUPPOrt.

Amy Mass

Also by Amy E. Madge

The Adventures of Kwungee and Uba Dooba Boy, published by Publish America

Memories of
My Parents

Amy E. Madge

Inspiring Voices®
A Service of **Guideposts**

Inspiring Voices books may be ordered through booksellers or by contacting:

Inspiring Voices
1663 Liberty Drive
Bloomington, IN 47403
www.inspiringvoices.com
1-(866) 697-5313

Because of the dynamic nature of the Internet, any web addresses or links contained in this book may have changed since publication and may no longer be valid. The views expressed in this work are solely those of the author and do not necessarily reflect the views of the publisher, and the publisher hereby disclaims any responsibility for them.

Any people depicted in stock imagery provided by Thinkstock are models, and such images are being used for illustrative purposes only.

Certain stock imagery © Thinkstock.

ISBN: 978-1-4624-0402-5 (sc)
ISBN: 978-1-4624-0401-8 (e)

Printed in the United States of America

Inspiring Voices rev. date: 10/31/2012

Hyde park 1944

Lorraine and John 1949

Contents

Memories of My Parents is dedicated to my late parents, John and Lorraine Madge, the best parents anyone could ask for.

I would also like to dedicate this book to my late brother, Bradley John Madge; to my brothers Kirk, Randall, and Craig Madge; to my sisters, Heather Hansen and Johanna Madge; to my nieces and nephews; and to the generations of Madges yet to come.

Illustrations

All photos in this book are from the photo library of the Madge family and were taken by John or Lorraine Madge or another Madge family member.

Introduction

After the loss of my brother and parents, with the encouragement of friends and a grief counselor, I started writing my folks' story. I found it therapeutic to express what I was feeling and to write my parents' story. I remember spending many nights in caregiver mode after working a full day. After getting my parents settled, I used to sit down and wish I had someone to talk to or material to read written by someone in my shoes. I still feel that way today.

Exodus 20:12 says, "Honor your father and your mother that your days may be long in the land that the Lord God is giving you." This verse is very powerful to me. Our parents are a gift from God. They should be honored and cherished. They are our teachers.

Lorraine and John 1958

1

Parents' Childhoods

My parents' story is simple. They were not rich or famous and did not dine with presidents or senators, but they were my parents—the most important people in the world to me.

I wrote down my memories of my parents because I believe their story needs to be told. What they endured in their marriage, the loss of a child, illness, and the longevity of their marriage are only parts of the story. I want their life here on earth to be written down and passed down for generations to come.

My parents were the best. I feel like I was the luckiest girl in the world to have had them for parents. I have always said, "I hope everyone feels the way I feel about my parents." They loved each of us unconditionally. Through them, I learned that love is not just a word; it means that sometimes you have to say no and stand up for what you believe is right even if that means standing alone. And most of all, through them I learned the importance of family.

They were part of the greatest generation. They married shortly after Dad came home from the war. Before going off to serve his country, he had slipped a ring on Mom's finger and asked her to wait for him. The rest, as they say, is history.

I have never seen another love like theirs—not even in the movies. They were truly soul mates. Did they always hold hands and kiss in public? No, they did not. Their actions spoke louder than words. They respected each other, and that was evident in the way the carried themselves individually and as a couple. Theirs was a silent love, and they had a strong admiration for each other. They were married sixty-three years, a milestone that unfortunately is not seen much in today's world. Was their marriage perfect? Of course not. They had their ups and downs like everyone else. But those hard times made them stronger. They grew to love and respect each other all the more by going through those times.

My dad, John Madge, was born on February 24, 1923, in Buffalo, New York, while his parents were immigrating to the United States. He just barely managed to be born a US citizen. He was raised in Hyde Park, Massachusetts. He was the oldest of four children. Because of the era he

Jack 1943

lived in, a lot of responsibility was placed on his shoulders. His parents divorced when he and his siblings were young. Back then, divorce was not supposed to happen. Before the divorce, Dad was an ordinary kid, hanging out with his friends, playing street hockey, and doing his paper route every day. Then came the divorce, and Dad worked to help support his mother and siblings. This was quite difficult for him—taking on an adult responsibility so young. He did it for the love of his family. My grandmother reluctantly had to accept the situation and let him do this.

She wanted her children to be kids, but with the times being what they were, she had no choice. At about the age of sixteen, Dad took a job with the railroad. I don't know how he finished high school along with working to help support his family, but he did.

Dad was raised to believe that men don't show emotion and are supposed to be strong. One story he shared with me took place when he was in elementary school. Dad was being bullied by a boy named Sammy. He came home crying, and his dad asked him why he was crying. When he told his father why he was crying, his father told him, "Boys don't cry." He was told to leave and not to come back until he had confronted Sammy. He left the house, found Sammy, and bullied him. Taking the lesson a step farther, he continued to bully Sammy. His dad found out what was going on, and he got disciplined for being the bully. It was quite a lesson to learn at a young age, one that he instilled in all of us: stand up for yourself, but do it in an honorable way. When World War II started and it was time to stand up and fight for his country, he did not think twice about it. "It was something that you just had to do," he always said when asked about it. "It was my duty."

My dad was definitely the stricter of my parents, so I found it quite funny to hear stories of Dad not always being on the straight and narrow. His late sister, my aunt Noreen, loved telling us kids how Dad and his late brother (my uncle Jim) used to horse around and get in trouble.

There is the story of Dad and his brother getting a nickel from their mom and being told to go down to the local store to buy a loaf of bread. My uncle talked my dad into melting the nickels down in one of their mom's frying pans, because they thought they could make two nickels. Another time, both of them got umbrellas and jumped off the roof of the house, because they thought they would float down like feathers. What a surprise it was for them when they both fell quickly to the ground. Thankfully, it was not a high drop. There is the story of how one night my dad wanted to go out and play with his friends after dinner. His dad had told him no; it was a school night. He wanted to go so badly, he snuck out to meet them. While crossing the street to go meet his buddies, he was struck by a car and broke his ankle. You can imagine the trouble he got into when his parents were told of that happening. The last of my favorite stories is one Dad told us. His mom was very much afraid of electric blankets. She wanted one but was afraid she would catch fire. My aunt Noreen finally talked her mom into letting her purchase one for her. On the first night she was to use it, my dad and his brother were in their room with a match. When she went up and got into bed, my dad and his brother lit the match and stood outside her room until she started to smell smoke. She called out to the boys and asked them if they smelled smoke, and of course they answered, "No, Mom."

My poor grandmother—sometimes I wonder how she survived all that.

It was good for us kids to hear that dad was just like any other kid growing up.

My mom, Lorraine Elizabeth Baer, was born May 28, 1927, in Brooklyn, New York. After the death of my mom's sister, Charlotte, in 1931, my grandfather moved his family to Hyde Park, Massachusetts, to start a new life. From age four, my mom was raised as an only child. When she was four and her sister six, they both came down with scarlet fever. Back in the 1920s, penicillin was not available. Mom survived; her sister did

Affectionately Lorraine

not. Up to the day she passed, Mom could tell how she remembered that after her sister passed away, the viewing was held at her parents' home. The department of public health put yellow tape across the door, because back then diseases like scarlet fever were highly contagious and that was the way to warn people. She also could tell how her mother took her every day to the cemetery to visit her sister's grave. She told me how she played around the headstones. She told me how much she missed her sister and how lonely it was growing up an only child. "That is why I always wanted a large family," she always told me.

Mom was a gifted pianist. She gave up going to college on a music scholarship to marry Dad and start a family. I loved hearing the story of her job working for the phone company. To make a call out, you always had to call the operator. She recalled those days with a smile and chuckle. Mom was a talker, and the hand gestures she used and the facial expressions she had were priceless. I can still see her sitting in her favorite recliner with her cup of coffee by her side, talking away with her hands moving a mile a minute and her eyebrows going up and down. She loved having us gather around and sharing these stories with us.

Mom was a very good student. When she moved up to Boston from New York with her parents after her sister's death, she went from first grade to third grade. She was quite proud of that achievement even into her adult years. She loved to tell us how, as a child when in elementary school, she got to go home for lunch. She very much enjoyed walking with her girlfriends back and forth to school. Through her own admission, her parents doted on her and tried to give her every thing she needed (but not everything she wanted). As she grew into a teenager, her parents decided to send her to a private girls' school in Boston. Being a teenager, that did not sit well with her. "Can you imagine that?" she used to say to me. "Being a teenage girl and *no* boys in school!" She survived, however, "and of course meeting your father closed my eyes to all other men," she said with a smile. She loved her friends, and she enjoyed going to shows in Boston with her friends and her mom.

Her parents were very protective of her, especially after her sister, Charlotte, passed. Mom told us she found their over protectiveness, holding on too much, and not letting her stay out late difficult at times, but she realized most of it was due to her parents losing her sister at such a young age. They were afraid of losing her too. "My parents were wonderful people," she would say. With pride, she told us the story of her father walking the streets during the great depression looking for work. He found a wallet with some money in it. Out of desperation, he kept the money so he could buy some food for his family. He wrote the owner of the wallet asking for forgiveness. "I had to feed my family," he said. She always said, "I remember my parents giving me food to eat. They ate nothing; there was only enough for me."

Mom's faith was very important to her. She was a strong woman of faith. It was that faith in God that carried her through life's trials and made her the strong, wonderful woman and mom she was. She faced every trial and tribulation head on. The disappointments and set backs that are part of life she believed were part of God's plan for us. "If it is meant to be, it will be," she always told us. "God never gives us any more than we can handle," she would tell me. She believed God never closed a door without opening another. I was always amazed at how she carried herself—always the lady, but if anyone ever hurt or went after anyone in her family, especially her children or grandchildren, the momma bear protecting her cubs would come out. She would defend and stand up for her children no matter what. Even if we were wrong or did something wrong, she was our mom and would stand by us. I remember once when I was in kindergarten, after school my next-door neighbor and I went down the street, opened a neighbor's mailbox and took out her mail, sat on the ground, and opened it. When my mom realized what we had done, she chastised us, told us why it was wrong, and marched us down to the neighbor's house, mail in hand, and explained to her what we had done. The neighbor, as you can imagine, was not happy, but seeing our ages, she accepted our apology. As she started to lecture us, my mom said, "They have been told what they did was wrong and will not do it again."

There is also the story of two of my brothers accidentally lighting a fire in the field behind our house when they were in second and third grade. Mom faced the fire department head on, and although my brothers were wrong to have been playing with matches, she was there for them. She was the most amazing woman I have ever known.

As a Couple

Wedding day

My parents met at Christ Church in Hyde Park, Massachusetts. Mom was about ten and Dad about thirteen. Dad told me he fell in love with Mom the minute he saw her in a church play. "She was so beautiful," he would always tell me while recalling that story. Dad was also my grandparents' paper boy. He was about eleven, and Mom must have been about seven or eight years old. Growing up, he took great pleasure in telling all us kids that Mom used to great him at the door to get the paper from him and tell him, "I am going to marry you, paper boy." No matter how many times he told us that story, we always loved hearing it. And every time, it always got a rise out of Mom. Their first date was in June of 1941. Dad always said he knew Mom was the one for him. When it was time for him to go off to war, he asked Mom to wait for him. Of course she said yes. While he was away, she wrote him every day, and he her. They were married April 21, 1946, after Dad got home from the war. Mom was eighteen and Dad twenty-two. Dad was in World War II in the US Army Air Corps, and he was darned proud of it. Their first apartment was in Dorchester, Massachusetts. I remember Mom telling me the apartment did not have a shower and they had to go to her parents' house to shower. They lived in Dorchester for four years. When it was time to start the family and they had saved enough money, they moved to Westwood, Massachusetts. That was in 1950. Mom wanted to be out of the city and in the suburbs to raise her family. They would remain in Westwood for the rest of their lives, moving only once to a bigger home to accommodate their growing family.

Easter Sunday 1949

$\S 3$

Creating a Family

M^y oldest brother, Bradley John, was born in November of 1950.

Lorraine and Bradley 9 months

They would go on to have six more children, the youngest Johanna Lorraine in March of 1967.

Brad, Randy, Kirk and Heather

The family Madge

My parents both worked very hard to give us the best and offer us the opportunities they did not get as children. Dad worked days and went to school nights to further his education. He graduated from Northeastern University in Boston and became an appraisal engineer. He got a job with a great company in a nearby town and worked his tail off to climb the ladder. He joined the ASA (the American Society of Appraisers) and even served a term as president of the ASA. Mom worked when she could to help out. Both my parents were children of the Great Depression. They told us kids all the time they never wanted any of us to go through what they did.

At times, things were difficult for them; raising seven children was hard. Through these hard times, they always put our needs above their own. Dad traveled a lot with his job. Sometimes he was gone for six weeks at a time. He would come home for a couple of weeks and then go on the road again. During those times, my mom was both mother and father to seven children. I remember her looking very tired and burnt out. I don't know how she did it. She never complained. She kept the house going and kept us all on our toes. I remember that on school mornings we got up in shifts—the older kids first, followed by the younger ones. Breakfast seemed like an assembly line. I still remember standing in the hallway wanting to run out the door with my older brother to the bus stop, but Mom was still braiding my hair. I can still see my mom wearing the same old ragged house dresses so the money could go to feed and clothe us. I remember quite clearly as a young child being at church with my family and going up for communion. While kneeling at the altar, I noticed holes in the bottoms of Dad's shoes. They never complained.

My parents made time for family and always did things with us. Sundays were always reserved for family. It was a day for us to be and eat together. We would go to church, come home, have Sunday dinner, and then do some kind of family activity involving us all being together. I remember every Sunday afternoon after Sunday dinner all of us piling into the old station wagon and going for the Sunday drive. Sometimes it was a drive down to Cohasset to visit Dad's brother and his family or just a drive in the car to be together as a family. The family vacations were always the best. My parents worked very hard to give us quality family time during our great vacations, providing wonderful memories that persist to this day. Goose Rocks Beach in Kennebunkport, Maine, became our favorite summer retreat and home. My parents started going there in 1955, and the rest is history. My parents had no idea what a beautiful seed they had planted in each of their children's souls by starting to go there. It is a place like no other, the Madges' piece of heaven.

A summer vacation is not complete with out getting to Maine. We all have a lifetime of memories at the magical place. It is a place where we made lasting friendships and memories, a place where, as a family, we could forget about school, work, and family problems and just enjoy each other. It was a place where I saw Dad *really* relax. We all still go their to this day. The love for that beach has been passed on to the grandchildren. I think they love it as much as we do. The last time I got Dad up to Goose Rocks Beach, Dad turned to me and said, "Your mother and I did good in introducing you all to this beach. It makes me so happy to see you all still enjoying it as much as you did as kids." A lasting memory as a child on vacation at Goose Rocks Beach, Kennebunkport, Maine, is Dad grabbing the movie camera and having us all walk down the beach toward the water holding hands. When Dad said to, we all turned around and waved to him.

Our holiday memories will always be special too. My parents were great at making the holidays the best ever. The trim-the-tree party before Christmas, decorating the house, spraying the fake snow on the windows, and making the house Christmas like and warm and cozy and getting us all prepared for Santa are such comforting memories. As children on Christmas morning, like all children, we could not wait to go downstairs and check under the Christmas tree to see what Santa had left us. Dad would always tell us we had to stay in bed until at least nine o'clock. It was such torture waiting. I remember my younger sister and me going into our brothers' room and hanging out with them waiting and waiting the few hours until nine. As children, the wait seemed to take forever.

Of course, to torture us more, he would take his time getting out of bed and then getting his movie camera ready. He always had to be the first one downstairs to get the lighting just right for his filming. Of course, he took extra long to drive us all the more insane. When he was finally ready to have us fly downstairs and run around the corner, before he gave the okay to come down, he would say, "Santa didn't come." We, of course, knew he was saying that to get us all going, but as the years went by we came to expect him to say it, and he never disappointed us.

More of my favorite childhood Christmas memories include falling asleep listening to Mom playing Christmas carols on the piano, Dad bringing out the movie camera and filming us hanging our Christmas stockings over the fireplace, and singing carols around Mom playing the piano. Of course, it did not take long for my brother and me to figure out there was no sound in Dad's movies, so we moved our mouths like we were really singing! Oh, how I laugh watching that movie to this day. As we grew older and got too old for singing, we had our annual decorate-the-Christmas-tree party. Mom made that a family tradition. She tied that in with my sister Heather's birthday celebrations, as her birthday falls near Christmas.

When the grandchildren came along, they grew to love and look forward to it as well. Every year, she gave them their own ornament for their own Christmas tree. Even as they grew, they always made it to Nana's to decorate the tree and get their ornaments. Mom so loved that. It would make her happy to see some of those ornaments are still around and are pulled out every year and hung on their trees.

My parents were even daring enough to drive cross country to California with six kids! I still can't believe that one! My youngest sister, Johanna, was not born yet, so I was the baby. I don't remember any of the trip, but my older brothers and sister took great pleasure in telling me the story of how I threw my rubber pants out the window and how, after we had stopped at the Grand Canyon to bask in its beauty, when it came time to get back in the car, I screamed, "No more car!"

One memory they both enjoyed sharing took place on a Thanksgiving road trip down to Washington DC to visit Dad's sister and her family for the holiday. My sister Johanna was just a baby, and they had set the cradle up in the back. They stopped to fill the car with gas, and the gas attendant looked at the car full of kids and asked my parents if they lived in the car! While in DC, our parents took us to the White House, where my brother could not understand why the guard would not let us through the gate to the lawn. I remember missing the bus to take us back to our aunt's house and all walking back to her home. We were pooped but had a good laugh about it.

They made it through the hard times. Mom went back to work to help with the bills for a few years until Dad got his promotion as an appraisal engineer and things got more comfortable. Even when things got more comfortable, they always lived within their means and taught all of us how to live within our means and to respect money, not to abuse it. I am not saying we are perfect, but the right values were definitely instilled in us.

Our parents instilled in all of us the importance of family. As we grew up, married, and had children of our own, this was passed on to the next generation. Mom became the glue that kept our family together. She used any excuse to get the family together. She loved the holidays, spoiling her grandchildren, and just having the family around her. Mom was in her element when her family was around her. As long as Mom was happy, Dad was as well.

Dad enjoyed having the family around as well. He was not as vocal about it, but he enjoyed it. An example of Dad's love for family and the legacy he passed on is about an old crow named Herman. When we were all small children and in school, at the supper table every night Dad would go around the table and ask each one of us how school was and what we had done at school that day. What we didn't realize was that when he came home from work, he asked my mom what had happened during the day and what we had told her about school. When it came time for each of us to answer, he would say, "Herman told me that happened, and he also told me what you did," and he would fill in the blanks by saying what my mom had told him earlier. We were always amazed and truly believed that Herman the old black crow was real and could talk to Dad. Herman was passed on to each of us, starting with Brad and ending with Johanna. When we all out grew Herman, we had and still do have quite a few laughs about it. Herman was started again when the grandchildren came along and started school. They too were amazed that Poppa knew what had happened at their school from an old crow named Herman. They were unaware, of course, that Dad was being filled in by their parents.

One story that is truly amusing is what my nephew Nolan said out of frustration to his dad after Poppa told him what Herman had told him of a playground incident at Nolan's school. After being totally amazed and flustered that Dad knew what had happened, he looked at his dad (my brother) and said, "Is Herman the same crow that used to tell Poppa what you did at school?" Maintaining a straight face, my brother replied, "Yes, Nolan," then Nolan very seriously added, "When is that bird going to die?" That is a story that always amused Dad and I am sure will be passed on to the next generation.

Mom and Dad always said their greatest achievement was their family. They meant every word of it.

4

My Brother's Passing

Though God brings grief, he will bring compassion, so great is his unfailing love, for he does not willingly bring affliction or grief to the children of men.

—Lamentations 3: 32–33

In October of 2005 came a day that changed our family's lives forever and one that we will never forget. My oldest brother, Bradley, passed away suddenly and unexpectedly.

Brad and Trevor

He was teaching a class at school and went in for a break and passed away in the teachers' room, just like that. There was no warning. God just decided it was time to call him home. That day was one of the worst of my life. I will never forget getting that call and rushing home to be with my parents. I pulled into the driveway to see Dad standing in the driveway, tears streaming down his face. I got out of the car and ran toward him. He turned and looked at me and said, "My goober is gone." Bradley was the first born and my dad's first son; he always referred to him as his goober.

I ran to hug him, and he told me to go be with my mother. I ran into the house and saw my mother sitting in shock in her chair in the kitchen. I ran and hugged her tight. She cried like I had never heard her cry before. She just kept saying, "My baby, my baby."

One by one, my siblings arrived. We comforted each other and especially our mom.

We drove out to be with my sister-in-law and her children. I was amazed at my parents' strength and the comfort they showed to my brother's wife and his two children. After my brother was buried, I rode back with them in the limo. I sat beside Mom, holding her hand. She just kept saying she did not want to live anymore. I told her she had to, for my bother's wife, for his children, and for the six other children she still had. Dad was very quiet. I saw tears streaming down his face. He was seated on the other side of Mom. He was clutching her hand with all his might. He could not talk about it. My parents' lives were forever changed from that day on. They would never recover from the loss of their first-born child.

❦ 5 ❦
My Mother's Passing

I am feeble and utterly crushed; I groan in anguish of heart. All my longings lie open before you, O Lord; my signing is not hidden from you. I wait for you O Lord; you will answer O Lord my God.

—Psalm 38 8–19, 15

Nana and Geoffrey

My beautiful mother, Lorraine Madge, passed away on April 22, 2009. She was my best friend, my rock, and my inspiration. I love and miss her with all my heart and soul. I was her primary caregiver for the last three years of her life. Mom had a rare fungal disease that traveled through her blood stream and settled on her aortic valve. She had a quadruple heart bypass surgery along with a valve replacement in June of 2004. She came through that surgery and was doing quite well until October of 2005, when my oldest brother, Bradley, passed away. It was a shock to all of us, especially my parents. I am not a parent, but I know the pain of missing my brother. I can't even begin to imagine the pain a parent must feel in losing a child.

About a year later, Mom became very ill. We could not figure out what was wrong with her. She had high fevers, chills, and vomiting. After a month of being in the hospital and enduring tons of testing, it was determined that a fungal infection had somehow entered her blood stream and attached itself to her artificial heart valve. The first solution the doctors arrived at was to conduct surgery again to replace the infected heart valve. The heart surgeon who did the first surgery did not agree with that solution—the first operation had taken a lot out of Mom, and the condition of her heart made her chances of survival very low. A team of infectious disease physicians was assembled to try to find a medication to put the fungus into remission. After about a month of testing, Mom produced two negative blood cultures. The doctors agreed that she should go to a short-term rehab facility for IV therapy to finish administering the medications. The doctors concluded that the only way for her to go home was for me to become her primary caregiver and learn to administer her IV medication. I did not hesitate one moment to do this for her—this was my mom who had done so much for me, and I would have done anything for her. Mom had a PICC line inserted into her arm, and the VNA came out to the house to train me so I would know how to properly administer her medications. She came home and endured six weeks of IV therapy. The medication she was getting was so strong she had to have blood work done frequently to check her kidney and liver function levels along with blood cultures to make sure the fungus was still in remission. She also had to have blood transfusions due to her blood count/potassium getting so low. She fought like a warrior and made it through round one! She was officially in remission. She was told she would have to take an oral antifungal pill for the rest of her life.

Two more times Mr. Fungus reared his ugly head and forced Mom to repeat the same ordeal. Each course of IV therapy got longer. The last course took eight weeks, bringing us right up to Christmas. Each session took more and more out of her. She got weaker and weaker, yet she rarely complained. Her last summer with us, she wanted to go to Maine for vacation so badly to see everyone she hid from us how awful she was feeling to make the trip. She was so weak at the end of the day my brothers had to carry her out to my sister's car to go home. The antifungal mediation was taking its toll on her and breaking down her body and strength. Some nights, she was so sick she could not make it upstairs to go to bed and ended up sleeping in her chair. On those nights, I would sleep downstairs on the coach beside her in case she got sick in the middle of the night. We called these nights our sleepovers. Most of those nights, we just talked the night away. It was as if she knew she would soon be going home to God. She kept thanking me for being there for her and sacrificing so much for her. I told her it was my turn to be there for her as she had been there so many times for me.

On March 13, 2009, Mom began her final journey. She was admitted into the hospital after going into diabetic shock. It was determined that the fungus was back, and all the treatment with the antifungal medications had taken its toll on her body and organs. She was in renal failure. She was in a new hospital closer to home. A new team of doctors was assembled. This team was incredible; they attacked Mom's illness like warriors. Their goal was to get Mom stronger, get the fungus into remission, and get her back to Boston to see a new heart surgeon who said he would possibly consider doing valve replacement surgery if she got stronger. Mom agreed to try dialysis three times a week to help her kidneys. She made it through the surgery to have the shunts put in her neck for the dialysis treatment. The plan was to send her home and take her to the dialysis center for treatment for several weeks. She was so excited to be coming home. She was like a child on Christmas morning.

As fate would have it, getting out of the car in the driveway, she fell and broke her leg in two places. She did not want to go back to the hospital; she had just gotten home. We called the fire department to help get her upstairs and into her recliner. They advised her to go back to the hospital, but again she refused. She tried making it through the night, but the pain was too much. She ended up back in the hospital early the next morning. She was in bad shape—her body was beginning to shut down. I had to start preparing myself for the fact that I was going to lose my beautiful mother. She tried enduring dialysis treatment in the hospital, but it was becoming too much for her.

One morning, the nurses from the hospital called us. Mom was refusing treatment. She did not want dialysis any more—she had had enough. We rushed to the hospital to her room. When we entered her room, she looked at us with tears in her eyes and said, "I am sorry." She was ready to go home to God, her parents, her sister, and my brother. We arranged for her to come home with hospice. She was happy to come home to pass on her own terms in the house she loved so much, the place where she had raised her family, with the love of her life and her family by her side. It was the place where her life with my dad had begun. She met with me and my siblings individually and talked with each of us. She told me how much she loved me and always would and made me promise to make a life for myself. She told me she could never repay me for taking care of her and not letting her go into a nursing home, the thing she feared most. She said, "God gave you to me and your father for a reason."

Mom's last earthly gift to Dad was the best one of all. With help from the Lord up above, she pulled all the love and strength from her soul and celebrated their sixty-third wedding anniversary on April 21, 2009. How she did that, only she and God know, but she did it. Amazingly, she was even able to sit up in bed. She was alert and even held conversations with us. To this day, I am still amazed at how she did that. But what a gift for my dad! They sat, held hands, and reminisced all day about their life together and how they had no regrets. It was such a gift for us to see that—we got a rare glimpse of how they must have been as teenagers when they first met. My sister took Dad down to the local florist, where he bought Mom a dozen roses. He walked into the room with those roses in his arms with the biggest smile on his face. When Mom saw him walk into the room with the roses, she grinned from ear to ear. The most moving part of the day was when Mom turned to Dad and said, "I wish we were young again so we could do it all over again." With tears in his eyes, Dad said to her, "I would do it again with you in a second."

As the day was winding down, so was Mom's strength. I went over and took her hand and told her how much I loved her. I also told her how pretty she was. Mom and I had this personal thing between us; being as sick as she was, she felt ugly, so I always made a point of telling her how pretty she was. Whenever I said this to her, she always looked at me, smiled, and said, "Oh, aren't I?" I always meant it; Mom *was* a beautiful woman. This time, she smiled at me and said, "Oh thank you." That was the last conversation I had with Mom on earth.

Shortly after that, she became unconscious. Her last night on earth is one I won't soon forget. Her screaming and moaning still haunt me. It was as if she had one foot in heaven and one still here on earth. We could hear her talking to my grandmother and my brother. It was very intense—she would say, "No, no, no, not yet; I need more time with my family." She actually said their names. During the night, she took my hand and was acting like she wanted to sit up. I said, "Mom, what can I do for you?" She looked at me, pointed to the ceiling, and said, "Look at the bright light up there and big white man." Then a huge smile came to her face as she said, "Bradley!" Bradley is the name of my brother, who passed in 2005. I smiled to myself as I imagined my brother urging my mom to come on and be with him.

Mom passed away on April 22, 2009, at 11:38 a.m. with me, my sister, and Dad at her side. I can't begin to tell you how much I miss her. Not a day goes by that I don't think of her.

No one has fought his or her illness with more guts and determination than my mom. I was sitting on the couch with my cat on my lap. My dad had fallen a sleep in a chair next to my mom, holding her hand. My sister Johanna had gone for a walk, and my sister Heather was sitting in the dining room. We were all physically and mentally drained. All of the sudden, my cat sat up straight, looked at me, looked over at Mom, and jumped off my lap and ran toward my mom. I jumped off the couch and ran to pick him up, as I did not want him jumping on Mom. As I got close to Mom, I noticed her breathing was getting labored. My cat let out a meow that sounded very sad. I whispered to Mom, telling her I loved her and it was time for her to go home to God, his angels, and my brother. I went to get my sister Heather and told her I thought Mom was letting go. Heather came into the room, and my Dad woke up. He asked us if she was gone, and we said yes. A presence of love filled that room. Heather says it was Mom giving us all her love and saying good-bye. I agree.

My Father's Passing

Blessed are you who weep now, for you will laugh.

—Luke 6:21

After Mom's passing, Dad never fully recovered. In the weeks and months that followed, he functioned as best he could by putting on a brave face and doing his daily activities. He enjoyed having his family around him, but inside he had given up; his heart was broken beyond repair.

I remember the first time he had to balance the checkbook. Mom had always handled the money and paid the bills; now it was his turn. Out of frustration, he looked up and said, "Why did you leave me?" At night I heard

John and Wesley

him in his bedroom talking to Mom and crying and telling her how much he missed her. It broke my heart to hear that.

Dad and I became closer. We became quite a team, he and I. I saw a side of my dad that I never saw as a child. When I was a child, Dad was always strong and in charge and never showed emotion. Now he was a different man. He had lost the love of his life and his oldest son; his world had come crashing down. He was not afraid to show his emotions.

I had always been close to my mom, and when she got sick, she became the center of attention. Dad moved to the back of the dog sled, never complaining. I took for granted that he was the tough, strong one and was okay. Now I could see how wrong that statement was. We became the two musketeers. I think he became a little too dependant on me, but I did not care. We became buds. He was no longer driving, so he would wait anxiously for me to get home from work to take him out and do his errands. He started including me in decisions about the house and asking my opinion in general. My sister Johanna and I got him out and about and even up to New Hampshire to visit his sister Thea.

The first Christmas without Mom was the hardest. Leading up to Christmas, it was horrible. He could not hear a Christmas hymn without breaking down. I kept telling him we would get through this. He would manage to smile at me and walk away. At nights, I would hear him in his bedroom talking to her, telling her how much he missed her, and crying his heart out. It was gut wrenching. He was throwing more and more responsibility on me regarding the house, bills, and money.

About a year and a half after Mom passed, Dad discovered blood in his urine. I took him to his doctor, who referred him to a urologist. After some testing, it was discovered Dad had bladder cancer. He agreed to have the exploratory surgery to determine the extent of it but made it clear he did not want chemo or any radiation. "I have had a great life," he said to me and my siblings. He came through the first surgery okay. The biopsy confirmed bladder cancer, and the urologist assured us that although it was a very aggressive form of cancer, it tended to move very slowly in elderly people. He asked Dad to follow up with him in six months.

The next visit and surgery were much harder on Dad. He came through the surgery, but the cancer had spread more than the doctor had thought it would. This surgery took a lot out of Dad. I did not know it at the time, but Dad had begun his final chapter on earth. Problem after problem followed him, yet like Mom, he battled his cancer the best he could. In January of 2012, he became severely dehydrated. He awoke one night and was so weak he could not make it to the bathroom. He fell trying to walk down the hall. I heard him fall and rushed out of my bedroom to find him lying on the floor. He was so dehydrated and disoriented he did not recognize me. As I lifted him onto his feet, he looked at me straight in the eye and realized who I was. He told me he was sorry and was afraid of losing everything to a nursing home and not having any legacy to leave his children. That is the kind of dad he was, always thinking of his children and still wanting to provide for and protect us even as adults. I told him he and Mom had left us plenty and most of all their love.

Dad ended up back in the hospital in the ICU. He was in bad shape. He had aspiration pneumonia, a UTI, and sepsis. The odds were against him. They started him on IV antibiotics and fluids. The care from this hospital and the nurses was incredible. He referred to the nurses as his angels. He improved enough to be discharged to a skilled rehab facility close to home. The plan was to get him strong again and send him home with VNA care. He started out doing very well there. He gave physical therapy his best shot, and they had him walking the halls with a walker and even lifting weights in the weight room.

The last night I visited Dad in the skilled rehab facility, he looked great! He was sitting up in bed filling out his food menu for the week and was in good spirits. It was one of the best visits I had with him through the whole ordeal. We sat and talked and really enjoyed each other's company. The next day at work, right before my lunch break, I received a call from one of the nurses at the skilled rehab facility where

Dad was. She told me she had just called an ambulance for Dad at his request. His oxygen level had dropped, and he had a fever. Where I worked was right around the corner from the hospital where they were sending Dad. I told the nurse I would meet the ambulance and Dad at the hospital. I arrived at the hospital emergency room around the same time Dad arrived via ambulance.

I admit I was not prepared to see what I was about to see. I figured he would be put back on antibiotics and that would be it. The secretary in the emergency department gave me the okay to go back to the triage room where Dad was. I was met by the emergency room physician, who promptly introduced himself to me and brought me back to the room where Dad was. When the curtain to his room was drawn, I saw six nurses working on Dad, three on each side. One nurse sat Dad up to put leaders on his back. Dad's eyes met mine, and what happened then is going to take me a long time to get over, as I can still see it in my mind. Dad was gasping and fighting to breathe. The oxygen mask over his mouth and nose was full of condensation. He looked at me, very frightened; I could see the fear in his eyes. He reached out his hand for me, and I gasped and fought to hold back the tears. One of the nurses turned and saw me and motioned for the doctor to take me out of the room. The emergency room doctor escorted me into a conference room and asked me what Dad's wishes were. In his opinion, Dad was dying—his pneumonia was back, as were his sepsis and kidney failure. My head was spinning. How could this happen? It could not be true; I was not ready to be an orphan. I cleared my head and knew the most important thing I had to do was focus on Dad. I had to put his needs first, talk to him, and find out what his wishes were. I had a good cry, called my siblings to tell them what was happening and to get to the hospital, and then called my sister-in-law, who is an elder law attorney and known for her level head. She emphasized to me that talking with Dad and confirming his wishes was the important thing I should focus on at the moment.

I walked into the room, took Dad's hand, and held it in mine. This was important to me. My dad was a strong man, a typical World War II vet who had been brought up never to show emotion. As we held hands, I felt that connection with him that is so special in a father-daughter relationship. I looked at him and asked him what his wishes were. I told him what the doctors' prognosis was. They could start him on antibiotics, but in two weeks he would most likely be back in the hospital again. His blood work revealed he had bacteria in his blood again, and it did not look good for him. Dad looked at me and told me he had had enough. "I have had a good life," he told me. "I raised good kids who I loved dearly and felt blessed to have them love me." He wanted to go be with my mom and brother whom his missed so very much.

Summoning all the strength I had inside of me, I went out and told the doctor what Dad's decision was. My dad started on what would be his last three days on earth.

The nurses and staff at the hospital moved Dad up into a big, private suite like room. Dad was started on a morphine drip to keep him comfortable and was treated like a king. My siblings and I were all able to visit with him. He was in his glory with his children and some of his grandchildren around him. We reminisced about our lives growing up and most of all thanked him for the wonderful life he and Mom had given us.

Dad told us all how much he loved us and how grateful he felt to have us. He mentioned to me that he was grateful for the gift I had given to him and my mom—the gift of being able to stay and grow old in their own home, on their own terms, and most of all not having to go to a nursing home. I never gave any of this a second thought. I admit at times it was hard working all day and coming home only to go into caregiver mode, but it was worth it. I wanted to give them the dignity and respect they so greatly deserved. He even mentioned how much he looked forward to seeing and being with my mom and brother again. He told my sister-in-law that when he caught up with my brother Brad, he was going to kick his butt for leaving first. Through her tears and smile, my sister-in-law Leslie said, "Kick him once for me too."

As we were preparing to leave for the night, I said my good night to Dad. He looked at me with a tear in his eye and said, "I love you—take care of yourself please." I had no idea that would be our last earthy conversation. The next day, Dad fell asleep and remained in that state for the next two-and-a-half days. For those days, the family stayed with him as much as possible. We did shifts, as the room we had been given was big enough to house all of us. The nurses and other hospital staff were second to none during this time. They cared for Dad with dignity and respect. It was so moving to see. They talked to him when they combed his hair and washed his face. I can't say enough about them. They also cared for and looked out for us. The hospital supplied us with food and beverages around the clock, and the staff made themselves available to us twenty-four hours a day.

February 18, 2012—the day that my dad passed away. On that morning, I felt a sense of urgency to be with him. I can't explain why; I just did. My sister Heather was in the kitchen when I came down stairs and announced I was heading over to the hospital. She said, "Okay, I will meet you over there in a bit when I finish up here." I drove to the hospital, and when I arrived my two brothers were there in the room with Dad. When they saw me, they told me there had been no change—Dad was still in his sleep like coma. They told me that since I was there, they were going to take a well-deserved break and get a bite to eat and be back later. I sat down next to Dad as I always did. As I was making myself comfortable, my cell phone rang. It was my brother Craig, who lives in Pittsburgh, Pennsylvania. He had been up to visit Dad earlier, but due to family and work obligations, he had had to fly back home. As we spoke, I told him there had been no change and asked him if he wanted to speak to Dad. (The nurses and physicians who were caring for Dad had told us to carry on speaking to each other and Dad like we always did, because even though Dad was sleeping, he could still hear us—the hearing is always the last to go, so he could not answer us, but he could hear us.) I held the phone up to Dad's ear, and my brother started speaking. I know Dad could hear him, because as soon as my brother started speaking, my dad's feet started moving. His reaction was the same as his whole family spoke and said their good-byes to Dad. When my youngest nephew, Wesley, spoke, Dad's eyes, though closed, moved rapidly back and forth, and his feet started going a mile a minute. I just know he heard every word.

Shortly after my sister Heather arrived, she sat on one side of Dad and I on the other. We were each holding one of his hands. We could tell by his breathing that he was starting to deteriorate. It was obvious to me that Dad was not yet ready to let go. *Why is he hanging on?* I thought. The nurses came in, and they comforted us and tended to Dad. They encouraged us to keep talking to him like we normally would, although it was hard. My sister Heather told him it was okay to let go. When she was done, I told him it was time to go be with Mom and Brad and if he was hanging on for me, not to worry; I would be fine. "You taught me how to fight, Dad," I said. "I will survive." Shortly after I said this, Dad let go. He crossed over to be with Mom and Brad. He was gone from this earth. It was 4:10 p.m.

The feelings of loss, abandonment, being on my own, and being an orphan were overwhelming. We had been the three musketeers; now they both were gone. What would I do with out them? Fear and grief were overwhelming. I felt like my heart would explode. I remember standing in the hall of the hospital after Dad passed going through the motions of calling the family and funeral home and so on when I remembered the dreaded blue box! The blue box was a box of information Dad had been assembling for me since Mom passed. It consisted of what to do after he passed, who to call, life insurance and social security numbers, and what he wanted done for his funeral. When Dad used to try to talk to me about it, denial would take over, and I would cut him short and change the subject, because I did not want to deal with it. Now I had to face it. I have to admit, I smiled. Dad had taken care of me once again. Somehow, I knew I would be okay.

Dad was gone; his suffering and pain had ended. He was now with God, his beloved wife, and his son.

Lorraine and John at Kirks

I take comfort in that, yet I hate being an orphan—I don't like the fact that both my parents are gone. I am grateful for the family my parents created, the values they instilled in all of us, and most of all, I am grateful that they live on in me, my siblings, their grandchildren, and the generations yet to come. I would give anything for one more hug from Mom, one more shopping day followed by a special lunch, one more after-dinner evening chat with Dad, one more dreaded run to Home Depot for a gadget he needed. Most of all, I miss his advice, knowledge, and love. I would do anything for one more chat with my brother or a ride in his plane, something I am glad I let him talk me into. It is a precious memory I will always have of him. He was also a little overprotective of me growing up; that drove me crazy, but having never married and having no children of my own, it was nice having my big brother looking out for me. While the loss was still fresh, I could not think about it without crying. Now I can manage to smile. I'm not saying I don't have bad days. They still come. I still dread the holidays, their birthdays, Mothers Day, and Fathers Day, but I am learning to smile again, learning also to say, "Thank you, Lord, for allowing these beautiful souls to be part of my life for this brief period of time."

Kirk, Nolan, Cam, Jon, Vanessa, Randall

Craig, Jen, Geoffrey, John and Lorraine

Dad was buried with an incredible send-off by the US Army. I know he would have been so proud—a little embarrassed by all the fuss, but proud. He was laid to rest next to his beloved wife, right where he wanted to be. I can picture him, my mom, and my brother strolling around in heaven, catching up on all the news.

Not a day goes by that I do not think of my parents and my bother. I am such a lucky woman to have had them in my life. I look forward to the day when we are all reunited in heaven. It will be quite a family reunion.

The grief waves are hard—they come on without a warning and are heartbreaking. I some times feel like my heart will break … yet I go on, because they want me too and I have to. I have to fulfill my purpose and to make them proud of me. They would not want it any other way. I find comfort in the memories. That is something death cannot take away from me. I hold them in my heart. They are in me. They are with me and will always be with me until we meet again.

John and sister Thea

The Aftermath

As a mother comforts her child, so will I comfort you, says the Lord.
—Isaiah 66: 13

As I find myself starting to clean out the house my parents built and raised me and my siblings in, the house where they entertained their friends, and the place the grandchildren called Nana and Poppa's house, I find myself in awe of what their love created—this house, this family, and the families that will follow. I also find myself sad. This is the only house I ever knew. It is a part of them that I still have. While cleaning out an old closet, I came across my mom's old scrapbook she made as a teenager. It was so neat reading her entries, seeing her old photos and things taped to the pages that meant something to her. I felt like I had found a time capsule and gone back in time. I had a glimpse of what my mom was like as a child and teenager. I connected with her on another special level. Finding her high-school yearbook and seeing her hopes and dreams written down brought tears to my eyes. Her excitement about her life yet to come with my dad when he returned from war was evident from what her friends wrote to her. She loved my dad so much and could not wait to start her life with him. Oh, if this old house could speak, what stories it could tell!

Yet I know my parents want me to move on and be happy and make a life for myself. I promised them both I would do that. I am

37

excited and a little nervous about my next life chapter. I was expressing these feelings to my brother Craig several weeks back, and I think he summed it up pretty well. He said, "Amy, the stuff in Mom and Dad's house is just stuff; it is materialistic. You aren't getting rid of and leaving Mom and Dad. A part of Mom and Dad is in all of us and in their grandchildren and will be passed on to their great-grandchildren and the generations that follow. Mom and Dad will live on." Well said, big brother; well said. He went on to tell me the story of an afternoon when he was teaching his youngest son, Wesley, who is five years old, how to play catch. As they were playing catch, a big black crow flew into the tree in their yard. Wide eyed, Wesley asked his Dad if that was Herman. My brother answered that he did not know, but it might be. He said Wesley took off his baseball glove and waved up to the crow and said, "Hi, Herman. When you talk to Poppa in heaven, please tell him I love and miss him."

I can add to that story another sign my parents are watching us from heaven and letting me know everything is going to be all right—the story of a cardinal and a whip-poor-will.

My mother's favorite bird was the cardinal. She just loved seeing and watching them whenever they were in our yard. We have always had a lot of cardinals in our yard over the years, but since Mom and Dad's passing, we have had more than usual. When Dad passed this past February, I found myself alone in this big old house for the first time. One evening after coming home from work and having supper, I went to sit out on the porch to enjoy the beautiful evening. While sitting out there, I started to think about my future—leaving the house, deciding where to live—and it hit me, really hit me, that my wonderful parents were gone and I was alone. The grief and uncertainty about my future engulfed me, and I started to cry. I found myself praying to God and my parents for strength. I found myself weak with grief, feeling totally alone and frightened. Just then, I heard the beautiful call of the cardinal. It sounded close. I looked outside, and there was a big, red, beautiful cardinal sitting right in the tree outside the screen looking right at me and singing away! I could not help but smile and think of my mom. *How she would have loved hearing this*, I thought. Then I thought that Mom sent this cardinal to me to sing to remind me of her and to let me know things will be okay and that she is and always will be with me.

That cardinal has been out at the same place for weeks now. Every evening when weather permits and I go out on the porch to sit and relax, it is there. What a beautiful and special reminder of a mother's unending love for her child.

My dad's favorite bird was the whip-poor-will. He was fascinated by that bird and its unusual call. One late afternoon last summer (I didn't know that it would be Dad's last summer with us), Dad, my brother Kirk, and I were sitting out in the back yard enjoying a lazy afternoon when, out of the blue, Dad asked me and my brother if we remembered hearing the whip-poor-will calls in the back yard when we were kids. I answered no, and my brother thought he could vagely remember hearing them.

You see, when my folks first built and moved into this home, their house was one of the first on the street. It was quite a woodsy area. When I look at the movies my dad took of the back yard when they first moved in, it looks like they were living in a forest. One scene is of one of my brothers running down the back yard. It looks as though he is going into a thick forest. According to Dad, there was all kinds of wildlife here. Over the years, as the neighborhood developed, things changed, and so did the wild animals that lived here. He said when they first lived here, he could hear the whip-poor-wills every evening and early morning. He said he just loved listening to them. But as the years progressed and moved on, so did the whip-poor-wills. They hadn't been heard around here in years.

I had my laptop out with me, and I Googled the call of the whip-poor-will and was able to find and hear the bird's unusual call. I played it for Dad, and it made him smile. I hadn't seen him smile like that since before Mom died. It was nice to see. It was a nice afternoon. I am glad I got to hear what the whip-poor-will sounded like. Little did I know how much that would mean to me less than a year later. One late spring morning, I had my bedroom window open. I had left it open all night, as the night before was an exceptionally warm one. I was woken up by a strange noise. It was a bird call, all right, but I had never heard that kind of call. Then it clicked: the whip-poor-will! That was a whip-poor-will calling! I jumped out of bed and ran to the window. *Yes, I thought, it is the whip-poor-will!* I pulled out my laptop and Googled the whip-poor-will call again, and yes, it was all the confirmation I needed. Of course I could not see it, but I could sure hear it. I immediately thought of my dad, how excited he would have been if he had been there right then listening to this with me. I was happy and sad at the same time. I found myself wishing with all my heart and soul that he was with me. All of the sudden, through my sadness, I realized Dad was there with me! He had sent that whip-poor-will as a reminder to me of his unending love for me and my siblings and a reminder that he too, no matter where the next life chapter takes me, will always be with me.

Geoffery and Wesley @ my parents (their grandparents) grave

As I finish writing my parents' story, I realize more than ever how blessed I was to have them. The way they provided for, sacrificed for, instilled the family values in, and most of all loved each and every one of us was second to none. I know that they may not be here physically with me, but they are spiritually with me now and will be forever. They made me and shaped me into the woman I am today. They are both with and inside of me, and I am part of them. That is something no one—not even death—can take away from me.

Does it take the grief away? Of course not, but it does ease it some.

"Jesus said, 'Now is your time of grief, but I will see you again and you will rejoice, and no one will take away your joy'" (John 16:22).

Family

The following are eulogies written by family members and read at my parents' funeral.

Jonathan T. Madge wrote the following:

It used to be said when all the grandkids were around Nana was clucking. I did not hear this phrase until a few years ago, but once I did, I felt it was very fitting. Everything that happened within our family usually happened because of her. The family flocked to her like a mother duck. Birthday parties, cookouts, and especially the yearly Christmas-tree-lighting party—they were all because of Nana. Every year in Maine, it was a big deal when Nana and Poppa came to visit for a day or two. We all gathered around to have dinner with Nana and Poppa and made sure Nana got down to the beach at least once before she left. No matter the occasion, Nana was considered the guest of honor in my mind. She was always the first person you went and said hi to and the one to say good- bye too. Not because we were forced to—because we wanted too. Nana always made me feel special in her own way. She always knew what we were doing and genuinely seemed to care. I knew this because of all the hand-written birthday and holiday cards she gave me. Messing up her checkbook drove her crazy. It eventually became a running joke between us. There is much I am going to miss about Nana—how she held the family together and how if Nana was happy, everyone was happy. Most importantly, I will always remember how she always came to the door to wave good-bye when we were leaving. Nana, I love you. You will be greatly missed.

Jeremy Hansen wrote his eulogy in the form of a letter:

Dear Poppa,
I wish I could say this personally to you, but circumstances won't allow it.

Thank you for the family you created. Thank you for the care and support you provided for everyone. You set an example for many young boys and girls in that house through the years, and I truly believe it was a good one. I will remember you as a gentleman who carried himself with class. The proof of that for me is my mom, as she raised us and continues to raise others into better people through your influence as a father. I am sure you are proud of that.

You will not be forgotten. I am grateful to have you as a grandfather.
Love,
Jeremy

At Dad's funeral, my late brother's wife, Leslie Madge, read the following eulogy, which she wrote specially for my dad:

Good morning. My name is Leslie Madge. I was married to John's oldest son, Bradley, until his death a few years ago. I met John when I was eighteen and have known him and his family my entire adult life.

After I became a lawyer, John would always greet me with, "Good afternoon, counselor," or, "Nice to see you, counselor." Then, with a sly grin, he would pull out whatever political or cultural hot topic he had selected that day for my edification and lay it like a fat red herring right in front of me so he could torture me. And he did; I never failed to delight him by rising to the bait, and we would have spirited discussions about the topic *du jour*. Looking back, I am not sure whether he always believed in the positions he took or whether he said them merely for the pleasure of seeing me argue against them.

To the grandchildren, he was known as "teasing Poppa," and it was true. It was how he showed his love. And I am grateful his teasing extended to me as well, with our discussions of controversial topics chosen so he could see me squirm. I will always treasure these memories.

In the later years, when I learned not to rise to his bait, we became best friends, and we grew even closer with our shared grief in the loss of his first son and then his wife, Lorraine.

John's greatest legacy is the seven children he and Lorraine raised and the grandchildren that came after. Their love and devotion is evident in the unit known as the family Madge, and I am honored to be one of them. I will miss him terribly but take comfort in knowing he is reunited with his beloved wife and first-born child.

Conclusion

I would like to offer my book to readers out there who are caregivers, to those who work in nursing homes, to social workers and nurses, and to anyone else who is caring for a sick loved one. If this book can be used as a ministry tool or study guide, then my goal will be achieved. While I was caring for my parents, I longed to have someone to talk to or even some material to read. I just did not know where to turn or where to go.

I would also like readers to send me their stories. The healing and grieving process can be helped when we share our pain and stories. God wants us to help one another in his name. Let's start right now.

Psalm 38: 8–9 and 15 says, "I am feeble and utterly crushed; I groan in anguish of heart. All my longings lie open before you, O Lord; my sighing is not hidden from you … I wait for you, O Lord; you will answer, O Lord my God."

About the Author

A my Madge lives in Westwood, Massachusetts. She is the sixth child of John and Lorraine Madge. She was her parents' caregiver for the last several years of their lives. She was proud that her parents did not have to go to a nursing home and were able to pass on their terms. Caring for them and being with both of them when they passed was a gift for her. Her parents provided her with a wonderful life and up bringing For her, this was a small bit of gratitude given back to them for all they gave her. Amy is currently working as a medical secretary in a town near her Westwood home. She is deciding where to move and start the next exciting chapter of her life.

CPSIA information can be obtained at www.ICGtesting.com
Printed in the USA
BVOW080158301112

306860BV00003B/291/P